In Times Like These

DEVOTIONS THAT REVEAL HIS CARE, COMFORT, AND COMPASSION

EDWARD POWELL

May the Lord be the strength of your life and the passion of your heart!

Edward Powell

2015

Isa 43:1-3

Copyright 2015 by Edward Powell

"IN TIMES LIKE THESE" by Edward Powell

ISBN-13: 9781511830973
ISBN-10: 1511830972

All rights reserved solely by the author. The author assures that all contents are original and do not infringe upon the legal rights of any other person or work. No part of this book may be reproduced in any form without the permission of the author. The views expressed in this book are not necessarily those of the publisher.

Unless otherwise indicated, bible quotations are taken from the Holy Bible: King James Version. Copyright 1937, 1945 by the Oxford Press; The Holy Bible, New International Bible Version (NIV). Copyright 1973, 1978, 1984 by the International Bible Society. The Amplified Bible (AMP). Copyright 1965 by Zondervan Publishing House.

Table of Contents

In Times Like These 1
God's Providential Care 3
Why Me, Lord? 5
"It Is Not I, But Christ" 7
To Have Or Have Not 9
Born For The Valley 11
When God Reigns 13
"Prepare To Meet Thy God" 15
Yesterday's Experiences–Today's Reality 17
Our Finest Hour 19
Whom Do You Serve? 21
If 23
We Have This Moment Today 25
God's Workmanship 27
Christ In All Things 29
The Lordship Of Christ 31
A Victorious Spiritual Life 33
My Grace Or His Grace 35
Lonely? ... You Are Not Alone! 37
Sovereignty 39
The Eternal Fountainhead 41
The Set Of The Sail 43
He Knoweth 45
They That Wait 47
This Is The Victory 49
His Way 51
True Friendship 53
Contentment 55

Our Choice	57
Appropriate And Apply... Receive And Rejoice	59
Becoming	61
Together We Can	63
A Beacon Of Light	65
My Radiology Report	67
His Voice In The Wilderness	69
So Blessed!	71
This Is The Captain Speaking	73
How Are You Investing Your Time?	75
The Ways Of God	77
By This I Know	79
In All These Things	81
Burn Your Bridges	83
Rise To The Occasion	85
"Walk Before Me"	87
Every Thought Into Captivity	89
Good Or Best?	91
When Day Is Done	93
We Shall Behold Him	95
Doing Good Or Walking With God?	97
Rivers Of Living Water	99
Fret Not	101
Common Days And Common Ways	103
Work Out Your Own Salvation	105
An Amazing Design	107
Lord, I'm Returning Home	109
The Well Is Deep	111
My Perspective	113
The Temple Of The Holy Ghost	115
A Father's Love	117
Thou Art The Man	119
"Jesus Took A Towel"	121
Why Reconciliation?	123
The Discipline Of Obedience	125

Fear	127
God's Refreshing Waters	129
The Wonder Of His Presence	131
The Red Sea And Jericho	133
Christ ... The Defining Issue	135
My Conversation With Jesus	137
The Journey	139
"According To …"	141
He Was There All The Time	143
Embers	145
Walking In The Shadows	147
"He Wholly Followed The Lord"	149
"Rejoice In The Lord Always"	151
Hearken Unto Me	153
Show Me ... Teach Me ... Lead Me	155
Love That Knows No Bounds	157
God Is My Portion	159
The Choice Is Ours	161
How Then Shall We Live ?	163
The Surety Of Our Faith	165
I Remember	167

Dedication

To all my friends who have through the years been stalwart encouragers, faithful prayer partners, and stood by me in the challenging encounters of life. God has used many of you to challenge my faith and launch out into the deep waters that I may see the marvels of His grace. It was there these devotions were laid heavy upon my heart until they became a realty through His grace. He has done many things in and through me that were beyond my capacity.

A dedicated life reveals in so many ways what God can do when we surrender to His Lordship and Authority. Thank you for being used of the Lord to be a great blessing to my life! May His Hand give to you a portion of what your lives have meant to me as together we look to Him and will soon see Him face to face.

Acknowledgments

I want to thank Richard Maddox, President of Malekko Software Systems, for his perseverance and expertise in editing these devotions. He exercised much patience to have these devotions edited correctly in all of their aspects so they may be easily understood and a blessing to all who read them. He has done a remarkable job and I sincerely appreciate the time and effort he has given with such a gracious spirit.

Foreword

How to read devotions. You do not read devotions like a novel. Each devotion carries truths, precepts and principles from God's Word for you to thoroughly meditate on and apply to your life.

The challenge they represent is for the deepening of your faith and draw you into an intimate personal relationship with Jesus Christ, our Lord and Savior.

Think through the words written with an open mind and a receptive spirit as the Lord opens to you 'new revelations' of His love, mercy, grace and all He wants to do in and through you.

Find a quiet place free from distractions so He can encourage your heart, strengthen your faith, and challenge you to surrender to His Lordship. He will give you a passion to walk in His blessed companionship each day and take you on an exciting journey through life. Just get blessed as only He can bless you!

In Times Like These

God allows many things in our lives to awaken us to our needs as well as to reveal the greatness of His grace. We need only look through our past years and see the *"Hand of God"* manifested time and again to protect, deliver, afford us a refuge, and direct our paths in ways beyond our understanding. The ways of God are *"past finding out"* but always for our good and to draw us to Him and His glory.

Presently, we may say, *"In times like these,* where is God when I need Him most?" What *"times"* are you facing today that are trying, difficult, and wearisome? David experienced many such occasions that tested his faith and defined his trust in the Omnipotent One. As he dared to place unwavering faith in God, he saw the unveiling of His will and divine provision for him. Are the *"times"* we face bigger than His Grace and Sufficiency? *It depends on WHOM we trust!*

We face false accusations, the poison of an unforgiving spirit from family and friends, loss of our job, devastating heath issues, and a vast number of difficult circumstances that reveal *the reality of our faith*. Is God's presence and power less *in times like these?* Absolutely not! God provides His love and mercy to enable us the see the marvels of His infinite grace and to provide a peace that passes human understanding. When we open our hearts and surrender to His leading, He untangles the cords that bind us in the bondage of our dilemma. *These are the ways of God ...* **"in times like these."**

God compels us to go where we cannot see the way ... forgive when our pride says "*stand your ground*" ... humble ourselves and see God lift us up ... open our ears to hear His still small voice when those around us shout, "*Just do it.*" Know the inner work of His Spirit by letting go of our human capabilities and seek Him with all our heart. Witness Him leading us in the paths of righteousness for His Names' sake. *These are the ways of God ...* **"*in times like these.*"**

God's workshop is in the common ordinary things of life. He prepares us in the *"little things"* to prove us to be ready, willing and able *"vessels of honor"* when the crises comes. He works in our lives in the circumstances we are in <u>now</u> ... in prayer, reading His Word, faithful to each opportunity, seeking the leading of His Spirit in our mundane daily life, standing true to Him in our relationship with others in response to our walk in His companionship each day. *Then,* when we are tested with *"greater occasions of anguish,"* we will respond *in His grace and let His Life live through us. These are the ways of God ...* **"*in times like these.*"**

It takes the *"renewing of [your] our mind,"* determined discipline of our character, and the continual surrender of our will to His, for us to be strong in our faith and filled with His Spirit in an overflowing measure. The *"times"* we face can be demoralizing, discouraging, and defeating if we face them in <u>our</u> ability and strength. Going forth in His Sufficiency, these *"times"* are opportunities of His Grace to be *"more than a conqueror through Him that loved us"* (Rom. 8:35).

The formidable difficulties we encounter are limited by the measure that our hearts are engaged with the Omnipotent One. They form no barrier to the one whose heart is fixed on God. HE often allows trials to come our way to test our faith, establish our walk, trust Him implicitly, and glorify Him through them. To walk in His companionship by faith is to know the exceeding greatness of *His power,* the glory of *His presence,* and the sufficiency of *His grace. These are the ways of God ...* **"*in times like these.*"**

God's Providential Care

In God's providential leading, He exercises His *Will*, *Plan*, and *Purpose* beyond our finite understanding. We read, *"O the depth of the riches both of the wisdom and knowledge of God! How unsearchable his judgments, and his ways past finding out"* (Rom. 11:33). Why do you think we have such difficulty trusting God for the miraculous? The underlying factor is we discount the *supernatural nature of God*.

Many are the occasions where Christ performed miracles beyond the ability of man. One of those was when Moses and the children of Israel were forced to flee Pharaoh and his army. They were almost totally encircled and the Red Sea was starkly before them. In the eyes of man, their outlook was beyond hope. There was nowhere to turn from the vengeance and wrath of Pharaoh and his mighty army. **BUT GOD,** in His providential way, rolled back the waters of the sea and left them a dry passageway through which they could escape *"through the midst of the sea."* That was miraculous in itself, but take a look at Exodus 14:25.

I've never noticed this before, but in our devotional reading recently, this verse jumped out at me. Pharaoh pursued them with his army, chariots, and the officers over all of them. When all of Pharaoh's army was in the Red Sea seabed, **Note:** *"The Lord 'took off' their chariot wheels ..."* The Amplified version reads *"And bound (clogged, took off) their chariot wheels."* The NIV reads, *"He made the wheels of their chariots to come off."* Remember, Pharaoh took *"six hundred of his best chariots, along with all the other chariots of Egypt, with officers over all of them"* (Exodus 14:7). Then, *God took the wheels off of their chariots.* Try to imagine. Regardless of what man can improvise, he cannot overcome the might of God. God is Almighty, full of grace and plentiful in mercy. *"He is able to do exceeding abundantly above all we can ask or think through his power that is at work in us"* (Eph. 3:20). Moses said unto the people, *"Do not be afraid. Stand still and you will see the deliverance the Lord will bring today. The Egyptians you see today you will never see again. The Lord will fight for you; you need only to be still"* (Exodus 14:13).

Do you think God can take the wheels off of your devastating need? **Yes He Can.** *"How unsearchable are his judgments and his ways past finding out."* It is for us to enter into God's Presence in childlike faith and commune with our Almighty God who is the same *"yesterday, today and forever"* (Heb. 13:8). In the solitude of His Presence, He will faithfully put His loving arms around us and bring deliverance ... *as only He can*!

What is the Believer's foremost virtue that will bring about such miracles of His Grace? ... **<u>Implicit Faith</u> in our Supernatural God.** If you disclaim the supernatural nature of God, you have no God ... you limit your hope within the boundary of your own making, resorting to restricted finite resources rather than trusting the Infinite Power of God.

God wants to take the <u>chariot wheels</u> off of your oppressors, the frustration of your weakness and the limitation of your own ability. He wants you to trust HIM without reservation!

"The Lord will fight for you, only be still." God will take care of our bitter experiences and turn them to rejoicing, our weakness into His strength, and our finite foresight into visions of glory ... *if we will <u>get out of the way</u>* and let God be the Lord and Authority of our life!

Why Me, Lord?

I have heard these words many times from Believers when they encounter a devastating experience. I have often thought, *"Why Not."* Do we think we are any different than other people? Have we done anything to deserve His consideration or gain acceptance with Almighty God? I'm afraid we all must answer with a resounding, No. We don't deserve His mercy, grace or love. As David wrote so forcefully in Ps. 8:3-4, *"When I consider thy heavens, the work of thy fingers, the moon and the stars, which thou hast ordained;* **what is man,** *that thou art mindful of him? And the son of man that thou visitest him?"*

God's ways are beyond our finite understanding; who can know them? Matthew wrote of the providence of God when he penned, *"for he maketh his sun to rise on the evil and the good, and sendeth rain on the just and on the unjust"* (Matt. 5:45). God never promised that we would be exempt from difficulty, trials or afflictions. He did promise that *"My grace is sufficient for thee"* (2 Cor. 12:9). He will be the Source of our strength through it all. Whoever we are and whatever we have or hope in the future … *is by his grace and grace alone.*

"Why Me, Lord?" I think if we took an introspective look at our lives we would find many reasons *why* the <u>ways of God</u> are at work in our lives. His desire is that HE may give us His best … lead us in ways beyond our understanding; protect us from the enemy; be our Refuge. He will mold our lives that *"we might be conformed to the image of His Son"* (Rom. 8: 29). This is the plan and purpose of God for us. <u>Why Me?</u> Because we are precious to Him and need to go through this encounter to be a vessel for His glory.

How often we need to go through the refining process of God's Hand upon us: *"That the trial of your faith, being much more precious than gold that perisheth, though it be tried with fire, might be found unto praise and honor and glory at the appearing of Jesus Christ"* (Peter 1:7). In the devastating suffering that Job went through, his answer to it all was, *"But he knoweth the way that I take: when he hath tried me, I shall come forth as gold"* (Job 23:10).

Where is the *focus of our faith*? When it is on the encounter we face, Satan will cause us to question God, *"Why Me, Lord?"* We doubt His providential care and compassion. We seek to find the reason for our dilemma and a way to counteract its effectiveness. We look within instead of *"looking unto Jesus, the author and finisher of our faith"* (Heb. 12:2). We open the crack in the door of our heart ever so small and Satan infiltrates into our thinking and emotions to discourage, defeat and destroy us.

Believe, Appropriate and Apply the admonition of Paul: *"For the weapons of our warfare are not carnal, but mighty through God to the pulling down of strong holds; casting down imaginations, and every high thing that exalteth itself against the knowledge of God, and bring into captivity every thought to the obedience of Christ"* (1 Cor. 10: 4-5).

This is the victory we have in Christ. Then the *"Why Me, Lord?"* becomes, *"The Lord is my rock, and my fortress, and my deliverer; my God, my strength, in whom I will trust; my buckler, and the horn of my salvation, and my high tower"* (Ps. 18: 2). **Nothing lies beyond implicit faith in Almighty God except that which lies outside His will.**

"It Is Not I, But Christ"

(Gal. 3:20)

The most successful people are those who place great emphasis on preparation. They develop their life by building on the basics, the fundamental characteristics that underlie the goals they have set for themselves. To ignore effective preparation will simply result in a plan that will be exploited by our opposition to our defeat. We see this in every phase of life.

How does an elite athlete train to become the very best? How does a track star excel above his competition? The answer can be found in a dedicated emphasis on excellent preparation. The athlete not only develops a demanding routine to maximize his or her natural talent but also has the necessary determination to persevere in pursuit of their goals. Being the supreme victor in a contest or a remarkable person that stands head and shoulders above all others also exemplifies another factor for success: the importance of seeking to *conquer something bigger than oneself!*

Paul knew something about this. He wrote, *"Now every athlete that goes into training restricts himself in all things. They do it to win a wreath that will soon whither, but we do it to receive a crown of eternal blessedness that cannot wither. Therefore I do not run uncertainly, without definite aim. I do not box as one beating the air and striking without an adversary. But [like a boxer], I buffet my body, handle it roughly, discipline it by hardships, and subdue it for fear that after proclaiming to others the Gospel, I myself should become unfit, not stand the test and be unapproved, and rejected [as a counterfeit]"* (I Cor. 9:25-27). Nothing was to stand in the way of Paul's dedication and commitment to God. God's plan and purpose for his life was his supreme task. Everything else was subservient in his life.

We, too, are called to run a race. The degree in which we are dedicated and committed to Christ will determine how well we have run the race and traversed the journey of life. *It will be transparent in our daily walk, evident in our conversation and obvious in every phase of our life.* God has a plan and purpose for every Believer. The extent to which His plan is executed and found in performed action will depend on our receptivity and response to the Holy Spirit. He works in our life that we may surrender our will to the Authority and Lordship of Christ.

Paul knew that anything short of giving the Lord complete Authority in all of his life was to fail. That's why his testimony is so forcefully resounding: *"But whatever was to my profit I now consider loss for the sake of Christ. What is more, I consider everything a loss compared to the surpassing greatness of knowing Christ Jesus as my Lord, for whose sake I have lost all things. I consider them rubbish, that I may gain Christ and be found in Him"* (Phil. 3:7). Paul pursued with perseverance in the might and power of God to be *"more than a conqueror through Him that loved us"* (Rom. 8:35). He said, *"It is not I, but Christ"* (Gal. 3:20). The Lord was his sufficiency for every encounter.

Where do we stand amid such commitments and resignation to the Lordship and Authority of Christ? *It is not <u>who we are</u> but <u>WHO is the LORD of our life</u>?* **Our life becomes eternally effective when the fullness and adequacy of Christ engulfs our life and is the motivating and authoritative virtue that is controlled by HIS sovereign power.**

To Have Or Have Not

Life is a constant challenge as to where our priorities are. To "have or have not" is not the essential ingredient that gives unto us an effective and rewarding life. The initial craving of our being is to find satisfaction in what God put within our hearts in creation. *He created us to glorify Him and to enjoy Him forever.* Therefore, that fulfillment can only be found when our will and heart is surrendered to His control and authority. It is a matter in <u>Whom or in What</u> we place our trust. How blessed it is to have a heart that is entirely His. If we have much, God will enable us to sanctify our prosperity. If we have little, God will be our sufficiency and supply the lack of our need.

<u>To have much</u> places upon us the responsibility of properly evaluating how we view what we have and how we use it in the most rewarding manner. Our greatest joy is not found in our possessions but in an intimate personal relationship with Jesus Christ as our Lord and Savior. Great fulfillment is found in giving of ourselves and sharing our possessions with others ... to live outside the boundaries of our self-interests ... finding, in reality, the truth that *"it is more blessed to give than to receive"* (Acts 20:35).

Many who <u>have little</u> of the treasures of this world often find <u>the Pearl of great price</u>. Their life is not concerned with the gifts God can bestow but in the Giver Himself. They become occupied with the Holy One and the infinite love God manifested in sending His Son, our Savior, to pay the wretched debt of our sin in the Atonement. When we focus on the Majesty of God, we get lost in the wonder of it all. We stand in awe of His abounding grace. Our eyes behold the One who has promised to *"meet all our need according to His glories in Christ Jesus"* (Phil. 4:18) and trust the One who *"is able to do exceeding abundantly above all we can ask or think according to His life that is at work within us"* (Eph. 3:20). The focus of our strength and the secret of our resources are in the One who created it all and who desires to be the joy of our heart and the passion of our life.

It is not what we have but in *Whom we trust.* It is not who we are but *Who He Is.* It is not in expressing our will but knowing and living in His Will. We find our greatest happiness when we focus our life on others and not on the greed that engulfs our self-centered life. It is living outside the boundaries of self that seeks fulfillment in being used to encourage, up-lift, and bless others in their need, and open our hearts to His full and free access to all of our life.

If we *have much* and our life is anchored in Christ, it will be governed and controlled by His will. To *have little* we find our sufficiency in Him to meet all our needs. The secret of an abundant life is not whether we "have or have not" but to live under His Lordship and Authority where *"all things work together for good to them that love God and are called according to His Sovereign will"* (Rom. 8:28).

Such spiritual reasoning is not the result of <u>our</u> evaluations but the work of the Holy Spirit awakening us to the reality that sin has separated us from the relationship that God originally created us for: *"The natural man receives not the things of the Spirit of God: for they are foolishness unto them, because they are spiritually discerned"* (1 Cor. 2:14). The Believer, who is living under the Lordship of Christ, is enabled to discern the basic factors which control the *"have and have not"* attitude. It matters little if he is in either category because Christ is: the focus of his being, the strength of his life, the joy of his heart, the sufficiency for his every need.

Born For The Valley

I am sure many of you have experienced the grandeur and exhilaration of being on the summit of a beautiful mountain ... taking in the cool refreshing air, lost in the wonder of God's creation, a time of healing our soul from the pressures of life that leads us to think, *"Wow, wouldn't it be wonderful to have a house up here and enjoy this inconceivable beauty every day?"*

And then, *reality* sets in, and we realize we cannot stay on top of the mountain but make our way to the valley. Spiritually, it is a great refreshing time to have mountaintop experiences with God. But, God never intended for us to remain there. To behold the sunrise or sunset from such illustrious heights is incredible. They are moments of exhilaration and inspiration ... **but we were born for the valley.**

We were born for the ordinary commonplace circumstances that challenge our faith and put to practical use our relationship with God. Mountaintop experiences are wonderful and have their place in our spiritual journey, but our place of spiritual worth is *in the valley* where we encounter on every side people with devastating needs. Our vision must be that of sharing His Love and Grace with those who have heavy hearts, broken relations, abused and lonely people who need the *"touch of His transforming power"* in their life and have a personal relationship with Jesus Christ.

Do we understand the _mission_ God has for us? Have we contemplated what it means to *identify with Christ*? Are our desires centered in having mountaintop experiences at every turn in our spiritual journey? **We were born for the valley** where God can live His life through us to reach others.

O that our eyes would see from God's perspective ... a heart ready to respond to His leading ... and a life that embraces the vision He lays upon our hearts. There is a face on which there will be no smile unless you put it there. There are broken hearts that will never have the courage to try again, unless you give it to them. There are hard-pressed souls who will not get through another day unless you pass along a helping hand and a word of encouragement. *God has made you necessary* to help meet the need of many lives *in the valley*.

Being on the mountaintop is not to *teach* us anything, but where we open our heart to the enormity of His grace and let Him *make* us *something*: build our character with the virtues of Christ. Our lives are not to be founded on emotional experiences or maintained by mountaintop meetings, but on an unwavering faith in God's Word and a personal relationship with Jesus Christ through living in the might of His power. The inspiration of the mountaintop prepares us for *usefulness in the valley* where the needs are.

We may think that the <u>chosen moment</u> that God places in our path is *insignificant. Not so.* God intends it to be of *eternal value.* Responding to His leading, God uses that <u>chosen moment</u> to radically change the lives of those you help. The encouragement you give to lift others from heartache, despair and depression can be *monumental*, not insignificant at all. **God met a great need and eternally blessed a life through you ... in that <u>chosen moment</u> in the valley.**

"To spend and be spent for God" (2 Cor. 12:15) knows no bounds. This is not a burden, but a glorious opportunity to see the Holy Spirit use us to accomplish things far beyond our earthly capabilities ... **We were born for the valley!**

When God Reigns

Why should we be surprised, alarmed or filled with stress and anxiety when alarming situations confront us? These often come unexpectedly and with pressing needs, disarming demands and fearful situations that penetrate our very being. We turn to our friends for support, cry out in prayer to God, and often find ourselves desperately weak in faith. Does this not blatantly stand before us as we have sought to follow in faith and pursue His plan and purpose for our life?

Well we might ask ourselves the heart-searching question, "Seriously, does God reign supreme in our life?" What is your answer to this question? I would think, if <u>*God Reigns Supreme*</u>, then He is in charge of everything that comes into our life. If we truly believe this, then the alarming encounters and devastation situations have come "through His permissive will." He has allowed them. Why?

"The ways of God are past finding out" (Rom. 11:33). Who are we to question His plan and purpose for these "pot holes" in our spiritual journey? When <u>*God Reigns Supreme*</u>, even these detours He has allowed will redound to His glory. The Believer, whose daily standard is claiming God's irrevocable promise in Prov. 3:5-6, will rejoice in the reality of their faith in this blessed truth: *"Trust in the Lord with all thine heart; and lean not to thine own understanding. In all your ways acknowledge Him, and He shall direct your paths."*

He or she will say with Paul, *"Who shall separate us from the love of Christ? Shall tribulation, or distress, or persecution, or famine, or nakedness, or peril, or sword? No, in all these things we are more than conquerors through him that loved us"* (Rom. 8:35-37). Also 2 Cor. 2:14: *"Now thanks be unto God which always causes us to triumph in Christ."* And, these blessed verses in 2 Cor.10:4-5: *"For the weapons of our warfare are not carnal, but mighty through God to the pulling down of strong holds; Casting down imaginations and every high thing that exalteth itself against the knowledge of God, and bringing into captivity every thought to the obedience of Christ."*

This is the faith that is consistently triumphant <u>When God Reigns</u> in every phase of our life. Does such faith find its rightful place in our hearts when, without reservation, we *dare to believe and trust God* when "potholes" confront us?

O to lean on the ONE who longs to wrap His loving arms around us in this spiritual journey and prove Himself anew and afresh that *He is able to conquer every foe and empower us to be victorious in every encounter we face.* Plant your stakes of faith deep in the validity and faithfulness of God and His Word. This is our only course of action if He is to Reign Supreme in our life.

But how great are the results! How blessed to see Him do things beyond our capacity, to defend, protect and lead us ... Who is our ever-present Refuge, our Strong Tower, our Mighty God, and the One Who will faithfully lead us triumphantly in these questionable circumstances that seek our downfall!

<u>When God Reigns</u>, we are in His Hands. We are being led by the Holy Spirit and He will perfect, bring to maturity and completion, what He has begun. Put your faith on the line and see what God will do in and through you. *You can never attain what only God can give.*

A victorious spiritual life finds reality by a life **surrendered** *to God, a life* **controlled** *by God, and a life* **lived** *for God.*

"Prepare To Meet Thy God"

(Amos 4:12)

It's amazing how mankind, in general, has no concept of God and how He relates to us. They vaguely think there is an impersonal God somewhere but do not consider that *"all things were created by Him and for Him: and He is before all things, and by Him all things consist"* (Eph. 2:16-17).

The infinite, eternal, almighty and supernatural God is not in their consideration. The Satanic ruler of this world has blinded their minds and caused them to <u>reason</u> within their own finite understanding, which is incapable to conceive the greatness of God. They disregard the inspiration and validity of God's Word and reject any consideration of eternity or life after death. They live in the bondage of their own understanding, which has been perpetrated by Satan himself. *"Eat, drink and be merry"* is the consummate objective of their life. They are without hope, without God, and are unknowingly dominated by Satan himself.

Is there any hope for such a person? Not apart from the reconciling, redeeming grace of God. But there is coming a day when *"at the name of Jesus every knee shall bow ... and every tongue should confess that Jesus Christ is Lord, to the glory of God the Father"* (Phil. 2:10-11). *"Jesus said, I am the way, the truth, and the life: **no man cometh unto the Father but by me**"* (John 14: 6).

Man forever seeks to find another way apart from God. Why? Because he is not willing to surrender to the Sovereignty of God and His Divinely-Inspired Scripture. They pride themselves in self-independence and will not seek any consideration of Eternal Truth. Their attitude is "no one is going to tell me what I should do. I am the Captain of my fate," as they defiantly disregard God.

How does all of this relate to *"Prepare to Meet Thy God"*? It relates in a very important way. God has revealed in His Word that *"all have sinned and come short of the glory of God"* (Rom. 3:23). God says in the following verse that *"[all] are justified and made upright and in right standing with God, freely and gratuitously by His grace (His unmerited favor and mercy, through the redemption which is [provided] in Christ Jesus)"* (Rom. 3:24) (Amp.Ver).

In Amos 4:12, the prophet proclaims, *"prepare to meet thy God."* You might say, "How can I do this?" By responding to and obeying the Truth God has revealed in His Word, *"For God so loved the world that He gave His one and only Son, that whosoever believes in Him shall not perish but have eternal life"* (John 3:16). We recognize that we have been separated from God by our sin and now stand guilty before a Holy, Righteous and Just God. In confession and repentance we bow at the foot of the Cross and receive Jesus Christ as our personal Savior. *"For He (God) hath made Him (Jesus) to be sin for us, who knew no sin; that we might be made the righteousness of God in Him"* (2 Cor. 5:21). *"For **by grace are you saved through faith;** and that not of yourselves: **it is the gift of God:** not of works lest any man should boast"* (Eph. 2:8-9).

Believe that Jesus paid the debt of your sin. **Confess** your sin and **Repent**, asking His forgiveness. **Receive** Him as your **Personal Savior** (God's appointed way to be redeemed and reconciled to Him). On the authority of God's Word, He said, *"But as many as received Him (Jesus), to them gave he power to become the sons of God, even to them that believe on His name: **which were born, not of blood, nor of the will of the flesh, nor of the will of man, but of God**"* (John 1:12-13). This is how we *"Prepare to meet thy God."*

Yesterday's Experiences -- Today's Reality

What characterizes your spiritual journey in relationship with God? Do you look back at the exhilarating spiritual experiences you had when God revealed Himself in a special way to you? You were on the <u>mountaintop</u> spiritually, rejoicing in His grace and love to you. It radically impacted your life and you desired to be wholly His. The Holy Spirit prompted your walk and communication with others and your life was radiant with His presence. How wonderful those days were!

But how about TODAY? Do your past experiences act as a <u>crutch</u> to hold you up for today's confrontations? We cannot live on past experiences for the present or future, expecting God to act as He did in the past. *Every day is a new occasion and adventure to trust Him fully!* He is looking for us to <u>walk daily</u> in His Presence, relying on His mighty power for the challenging circumstances we face today, and appropriating His irrevocable promises that we might be *"partakers of the divine nature"* (2 Peter 1:4).

God wants to embrace our life with His virtues *Today* as He lives His life through us. We should seek to grow in grace that we may be *strong in our stand and vibrant in our witness*. Let the past be a springboard to move us forward and deepen our dedication and commitment to His plan, purpose and will for our spiritual journey.

It reminds me of marriage. The honeymoon was wonderful but we must face reality. However blessed it was, it will not suffice for Today. All the experiences of the unknown future will find its greatest joy not in us, but living <u>outside</u> us unto the Lord and others. We must cultivate, nurture, and develop a life united together and prefer the other more than ourselves (Rom. 12:10).

TODAY is given to us by God's grace. We did not earn it, cannot buy it, and, in His sight, do not deserve it. "All we are in grace is *by Christ*; all we have is *from Christ*; all we shall ever be is *through Christ*. We are empty, but *He fills us;* we are lost, but *He saves us;* we are naked, but *He clothes us*; we are helpless, but *He strengthens us*" (Dr. Herbert Lockyer). ALL by His infinite grace.

There are no short cuts to living <u>*triumphantly*</u> for God today. It is not a one-time attainment, but a daily surrender of our will to His Lordship and resting in His sufficiency. Through God's grace, He seeks to mold our lives to the *"image of his Son"* (Rom. 8:29).

It's amazing how God works in our lives when we get out of the way and surrender the control of our lives to His Authority and Sovereign leading. Seeking to know God means the persevering pursuit to *"abide in Him"* (John 15:5).

We need to start each day to *meet Him* in the secret place of His presence: to *know Him* in an intimate relationship, to *worship Him* in the beauty of holiness, and *walk with Him* in the blessedness of His companionship.

When Christ is on the throne of our heart and the Authority of our life ... **we will never be the same!** Our life will be an exciting journey each day as He manifests the <u>*fruit of the Spirit*</u> in and through us. Live TODAY in the reality of your faith firmly fixed on Christ. He will enable us to walk in the consciousness of His presence. How blessed! This is Life on the Highest Plane! **Dare to Believe ... Dare to Trust ... Dare to Walk "under the shadow of His Wings"** (Ps. 17:8) **Today.**

Our Finest Hour

Our life is a constant challenge to achieve, excel and clothe our character with those virtues that will inspire others and lift them above the boundaries they have allowed to discourage and defeat them. Many times we create our own distress ... we limit the power within our spirit to accomplish what is beyond our ability, and fail to exercise the *"will to win,"* whatever the encounter we face.

Complacency does not accompany the person who seeks to stand tall when others fail for lack of perseverance and determined purpose. There is always a price to pay if we are to achieve the high standard of excellence ... to press on when our most exerted efforts seem far from enough and to discipline our lives to sacrifice whatever it takes in refusing to give in to our feelings and emotions.

We find such virtues in men like Hudson Taylor, the humble dedicated Missionary that opened the doors of China to the Gospel. He found the secret: it's not determination or sacrificial endeavor but *surrender to the Lordship of Christ*. The truth that *"it is not I but Christ living in me"* (Gal. 2:20) became a living reality in every phase of his life. God worked in and through him in an inconceivable way.

*In seventy years, his mighty **faith mission** (a ministry without any financial support but childlike Faith in Almighty God) numbered 1083 missionaries, 1968 paid Chinese helpers, more than 2000 Chinese workers— who labored in the 250 stations, 1600 chapels, 11 hospitals and hundreds of dispensaries. 500 schools were erected and over a hundred thousand Chinese were saved: a trophy of HIS GRACE! It was **"his finest hour."***

David Livingston blazed the jungles of the Dark Continent of Africa. His legacy is found where the curling smoke from a thousand African villages testifies to his incredible ministry. It has been written of him, *"His spirit was given to Africa in devotion to the cause of Christ, as his heart was given to the African soil, which he so dearly loved, in burial."* This was **"his finest hour."** For nine months his body, from which the heart had been cut out and tenderly placed in African soil, was carried by faithful black natives to the coast. His final resting place was among the great in England's Westminster Abbey.

Such Divine achievements in the past few hundred years have been recorded from men such as Francis of Assisi, John Bunyan, Augustine, John Calvin and Kagawa who opened the doors of Countries and Continents to the Gospel. For those burned at the stake such as Hugh Latimer, Nicholas Ridley, John Rogers and countless others, we stand in awe and admiration. We also admire Count Zinzendorf, John Wesley, John Paton and innumerable others, to which the cost was never too great to pay, the sacrifice never too demanding to make, for their unwavering faith was never in question but was the watchword of their life.

Only Eternity will reveal the <u>*Heroes of the Faith*</u> who found their <u>**finest hour**</u> amidst the emissaries of Satan himself but triumphed gloriously through God's grace and power that honored their unwavering faith. To read through the pages of Christian history should challenge our heart to surrender to His Lordship and seek to be that *"vessel of Honor"* that characterized the lives of the stalwarts of the faith. Let us pay the cost, press on in spite of the circumstances and make whatever sacrifice is demanded without hesitation. May our lives reveal <u>**our finest hour**</u> to which our Lord is glorified and honored as HE lives HIS life through us.

Whom Do You Serve?

That's an interesting question. You might say, "I don't serve anyone." When you read God's account of man, He very clearly specifies **you serve either Him or you serve Satan:** *"No man can serve two masters: for either he will hate the one, and love the other; or else he will hold to the one, and despise the other. You cannot serve God and mammon"* (Matt. 6:24).

Unfortunately, man so often discards the truth and validity of God's infallible Word. He responds to his deceiving heart: *"The heart is deceitful above all things and desperately wicked: who can know it?"* (Jer. 17:9). He reasons within his own human thought and yields to the infiltrating ways of Satan who has blinded his eyes to the Truth: *"The god of this world has blinded the minds of them which believe not, lest the light of the glorious gospel of Christ, who is the image God, should shine unto them"* (2 Cor. 4:4).

He lives in the bondage of his own choice apart from God, condemned by his own sin and under the judgment of God. He has a biased attitude that condones his lifestyle and ungodly choices under the influence and control of Satan. As such, he *serves the god of this world,* without regret or remorse. When we compare our character with any other than God's standard, we will have a distorted evaluation of our self that is but an illusion propagated by Satan.

Mankind shuns being under Divine Authority. They want freedom... but on their own terms. They want happiness, joy and peace ... but seek them in the superficial allurements of our worldly system controlled by Satan. He craves a free spirit ... but lives under the insidious ways of evil that control his desires, infiltrates his morals and defines his life.

To serve God and have Him as the authority of our life is to have a receptive and responsive spirit surrendered to the leading of the Holy Spirit where HE has free and full control of all of our life. This is serving God and embracing life on the highest plane. Divine Truth must be an integral part of our life applied in every dimension of our spiritual journey.

The truth, principles, and precepts of God's Word are the foundation and building blocks for us to know and be led of Him in all of our life. Truth is transparent, profound, sincere and factual, with integrity and depth of character. There is no pretense or hypocrisy. It demands high moral standards that require us to surrender our right to control our life to the Lordship of Christ.

Such are the demands of serving God, being under His Divine Authority and walking daily with Him in an exciting companionship. **How blessed it is to serve God!** The infinite love of God will be the subject of our meditation ... the theme of our praise ... the object of our affections ... the joy of our hearts ... the strength of our life ... and the passion of our heart! What a comparison to the unbeliever whose life centers on his selfish greed and self-independence.

God has made a tremendous irrevocable covenant to all who will follow Him in childlike obedience and yield their will to His Lordship and Authority with unwavering trust. He has promised, *"You are a chosen generation, a royal priesthood, a holy nation, a peculiar people; that you should show forth the praises of him that hath called you out of darkness into his marvelous light: which in times past were not a people, but are now the people of God: which had not obtained mercy, but now have obtained mercy"* (1 Peter 2: 9-10). **Our life is eternally effective when the fullness of Christ engulfs our life and is our motivating power**

If

Someone wisely said, *"there are no if's with God."* When we are "abiding in *Him*" (John 15:5), He is in control of every phase of our life. Our life is in His hand. We are under His Sovereign Providential care. **The how, why, where, what and when is not our concern, but HIS.** When faced with life's challenging issues, His care, His Plan, and His Purpose will be manifested in His Time and in His Way as we dare to believe and trust Him.

Look at the magnitude of God's promise to us in Prov. 3:5-6: *"Trust in the Lord with all our heart and lean not to our own understanding. In all our ways acknowledge Him and He shall bring it to pass."* The penetrating question is, **do we truly believe this promise ...** or is it simply a verse *we wish* was a living reality in our life? Many refer to these verses with <u>wishful faith</u> but few <u>appropriate its irrevocable truth</u> and live in the reality of unwavering trust in His word to us.

So often we hear others use this incredible word, "IF." This simply reveals how shallow their faith in God really is. In our finite, unbelieving heart we think, "If this or that had been different, the results would have been so much to our advantage." In other words we're saying, "If we were in charge of that situation, I would have done it differently." Is this not the expression of our uncommitted heart that simply says, "I know better than God"?

Why is it so difficult for us to yield our will and surrender our life to His divine control? Why do we insist on trying to understand God's leading <u>our way</u> rather than submitting to <u>His Way</u>? The last citadel we are willing to yield is ... **to surrender the control of our will**

to God's divine control. That's why *IF* is a debating issue when we are not under His Lordship. We do not understand His ways, therefore we fail to trust Him fully: *"For my thoughts are not your thoughts, neither are your ways my ways, saith the Lord. For as the heavens are higher than the earth, so are my ways higher than your ways, and my thoughts than your thoughts"* (Isa. 55:8-9).

Why do we entertain such simplistic carnal thought? The answer is evident: ***We do not believe His promises nor do we expect them to be fulfilled!*** Is this not the reason so few see miracles of His grace being manifested in their lives? Is this not why so few see God *answering prayer* and moving the mountains of difficulty and despair? *Unbelief* underlines their faith and characterizes their shallow walk with God.

To the true committed Believer, God is not someone, somewhere out there but a *Living Indwelling Presence* in our life. We are the Temple in which He dwells. Our Heart is the Throne on which He reigns supreme in our spiritual walk. It's not for us to inject *IF* in any situation when He is our LORD. *"Thou wilt keep him in perfect peace, whose mind is stayed on thee: because he trusteth in Thee"* (Isa. 26:3). The measure by which we daily exercise childlike faith in our Almighty God, will reveal how great or how small our concept of God really is. True faith has no *IF*'s.

Many are reluctant to believe that God desires to be an integral part of every phase of our life. Faith should be the distinguishing characteristic in every Believer and exercised in implicit obedience. Its benefits are incalculable! Dare to believe, to trust, and to walk with Him in the consciousness of His Presence and in the reality of unwavering faith!

We Have This Moment Today

We live in a complex world where values and virtues differ in every direction. The perspective of so many is diverted, obscured, and without any sense of personal accountability. Many live in the *afterglow of yesterday* with its excitement, acceleration and fulfillment. They linger on life *as it was* rather than confronting life *as it is:* living in the past instead of embracing the excitement of living in the blessings of TODAY.

Others embrace what they anticipate *tomorrow will be,* always seeking what might be at the expense of living in the reality of today. They reach out to the uncertainty of tomorrow with an insecure foundation, *fantasizing the unknown* as if it were already in their grasp. Their focus is in a <u>*dream world of expectation*</u> while ignoring the course they are presently following ... instead of being strengthened by the might of His power in the inner man ... His Life lived through us!

Years ago I heard Doug Oldham sing a simple yet profound truth so many are missing today. The chorus says it all: **"We have this moment to hold in our hand. It falls through our fingers like grains of sand. Yesterday is gone ... and tomorrow may never come ... but we have this moment TODAY."**

How blessed to seize every moment TODAY ... to embrace those we love and let them know how much we appreciate all they have given of themselves to us. Share the joy of having eyes to see, ears to hear, a mind that understands and expresses itself in buying up the moment we have TODAY.

Reach within and find some way to let others know the incredible blessing of <u>walking in the reality of His Presence</u> ... embracing the <u>irrevocable promises of God</u> ... knowing the <u>peace of God</u> that fills our hearts ... the <u>joy of the Lord</u> that is our strength and the <u>blessed hope of eternal life</u>. These things we have TODAY! **Believe them ... Seize them ... Live them!** O that we might not clutter our life with the temporal and passing fantasies ... the shallow artificial allurements of the world ... the superficial friends that disappoint and discourage us ... but *fix our eyes on the FAITHFUL ONE, the Author and Finisher of our faith. The ONE who changes not ... the same yesterday, today and forever!*

TODAY is a new adventure, a new occasion for us to trust Him fully and see Him do things in and through our life that are *beyond our imagination and ability to achieve.* Each moment is precious; **it will not pass our way again.** May we possess and enjoy it ... maximize it to the full ... recognize the incredible blessing of <u>living</u> ... fill our life to overflowing with the blessed truth. God said, *"Fear thou not; for I am with you: be not dismayed; for I am your God: I will strengthen you; yea, I will help you; yea, I will uphold you with the right hand of my righteousness"* (Isa. 41:10).

Let our heart find expression outside of ourselves. Helen Keller so beautifully expressed this in her remarkable way, *"The best and most beautiful things in life cannot be seen or even touched ... they must be felt with the heart."* TODAY, may we lead with our heart ... our life will follow ... and others will be moved and touched by *our heart and life of love.*

We underestimate such a life, but when God's love flows freely through us, it finds expression in a smile you put on another's face ... an encouraging word that lifts them from their despair ... and a compassion that will move their heart! Seize the moment for His glory!

God's Workmanship

What an awesome realization! Few Believers have ever given serious consideration of this work of God's grace. They enjoy fellowship in the church, are active in participation of its outreach to others, and take part of their responsibility in the church's ministry. These are all commendable, but **there is something even deeper.** *It is opening up our heart and will to **God's workmanship**.* This involves entering into an intimate relationship with Christ whereby He has control and authority of our will. This resignation to His Lordship gives the Holy Spirit freedom to mold and make our life a *"vessel of honor"* that will glorify the Lord in every phase of our life. **We can never attain what only God can do.**

Michelangelo wrote, *"The grinding and sanding of the marble statue gives the beauty and smoothness that delights the eye."* The Statue of David, acclaimed by the world for its exquisite form, detail, shape, and artistry was the result of countless hours of meticulous work to perfect its beauty. There was much grinding and sanding to complete this masterpiece. It stands as a memorial to the dedication, perseverance and greatness of this classic artist.

Our salvation is the result of God's amazing grace, His everlasting mercy, and His infinite love. Having accepted Christ as our Savior we have been redeemed and reconciled to God ... **but there is more.** He has saved us that *He may live in and through us for His glory.* God wants to conform us *"in the image of His Son"* (Rom. 8:29). *His workmanship* will take us through the grinding and sanding process to *"purify unto Himself a peculiar people, zealous of good works"* (Titus 2:14).

We are often resistant to His Hand upon our life that seeks to bring to the surface the impurities and selfish pride that distorts our life and our walk. The sinful fleshly nature that has been ingrained into our lives for years needs to be exchanged for the <u>new nature</u> we receive from Christ at salvation. The *"old man"*, with all of its carnal desires and lusts, must be put off. Thus <u>God's workmanship</u> begins to bring to our attention the process that directs the course God takes to shape our lives and reflect His virtues.

God said, *"Be ye holy for I am holy"* (Lev. 20:7). Holiness is the result of <u>God's workmanship</u> as He refines and purifies our life. We will experience many trying confrontations that seek to bring us to our knees at the foot of the cross. These encounters will reveal the arrogance, anger, pride and self-independence that engulfed our old nature. The molding process of God's grace shapes us to reflect Him in our conversation, walk, and all of our life. Instead of being unconcerned and rejecting this demanding course of <u>God's workmanship</u>, we need to open our hearts, will, and life to respond with confession and repent of our apathy so His work of grace will not be inhibited. *"But he knoweth the way that I take: when he hath tried me, I shall come forth as gold"* (Job 23:10).

As a refiner sits before his crucible to remove the dross and impurities, so <u>God's workmanship</u> brings out the impurities in our life that displease Him. How blessed are the results when we submit to His mercy and grace. He develops in us the *"image of His Son"* that we may reflect the virtues of His grace. He empowers us in the inner man to be *"more than conquerors through Him that loved us"* (Rom. 8:35). **Christ was made in the likeness of man ... that we may be conformed to the likeness of Christ.**

When submissive to His work of grace, there comes ... a reverent declaration ... a covenant with God ... an unwavering trust in God in the quietness of His presence ... with a humble and contrite spirit. How glorious His workmanship!

Christ In All Things

What is your ultimate initiative as a Christian? Your answer will reflect the way you live and the priority Jesus Christ has in your daily walk. Many compartmentalize their secular life from their spiritual life. They make time for Christ, for worship, prayer, and service. After involvement in these responsibilities, they continue to advance their self-realization and pursue the fulfillment of their personal interests. This leads to the *enthronement of self* with all of its baggage and consequences.

The aim of the *spiritual Believer* is not centered in *self* at all, with its shallow enticements and illusive fortunes. Its primary premise is the same as Paul, ***"That I may KNOW HIM"*** (Phil. 3:10-14). Our aim as a spiritual Believer is *to secure the realization of Jesus Christ being the integral virtue and Authority **in every phase of our life.***

We recognize that the circumstances, situations, people, and whatever we face are either *ordained of God or allowed by Him*. We must *fix our eyes on Him* and see that these occasions in our life are the means of letting God do what is necessary to bring us into a personal intimacy with Him. *"See God in all things, surrender to His Providential Will, and God will make all things work together for our good and His Glory"* (Rom. 8:28-29).

Paul wrote, *"(For my determined purpose is)* ***that I may know Him*** *... that I may progressively become more deeply and intimately acquainted with Him, perceiving and recognizing and understanding (the wonders of His Person) more strongly and more clearly"* (Phil. 3:10)(Amp.Ver.). This is not something we casually *"go with the flow"* into, but a **deliberate calculated purpose of our will.**

We will, to respond in obedience ... *we will,* to trust Him fully in all confrontations ... *we will,* to open our hearts to the Holy Spirit and His work of grace ... *we will,* to *"deny ourselves, and take up **our cross** daily, and follow Him"* (Luke 9:23). This is a commitment and promise between God and us. ***Our will*** is the controlling factor of our character. It must be exercised and committed to God so He can conform us into the *"image of His Son"* (Rom. 8:29).

God wants to bring us back to that which He created us for. When we rely on anything but God, we are putting those things between God and us. This automatically puts God *"on the shelf"* until we realize we are not in unity with Him or His will. Our attitude, motives, self-interests, desires or purpose, when activated by *self*, distorts our full view of Him. To see Him is to come to know Him in all His fullness and majesty. Our focus and commitment must be unhindered if we are to respond with our whole being. There must not be any impediments that hinder Him filling us with the fullness of Himself.

Our spiritual life finds **completeness and reality** *when* **Christ is in all things** ... *by our life* **surrendered to God** ... *by our life* **controlled by God** ... *and by our* **life lived for God**. David loved to worship in the Temple, to be in the Presence of God. He was overwhelmed with *All God Is.* He could not find adequate words to express all that was in his heart, so he shouts forth, *"Bless the Lord O my soul and* **all that is in me,** *Bless His Holy Name"* (Ps. 103:1). May this be the expression of our hearts and the joy of our life.

Our life becomes **eternally effective** *when we yield our entire being to the fullness of the Holy Spirit ... when the adequacy of Christ engulfs our life in all of His sufficiency ... and He is the motivating power* **in every phase of our life.**

The Lordship Of Christ

We hear very little about the *"Lordship of Christ."* Many have no idea what it means to have Christ as the Authority of every phase of their life. As a Believer, they have never responded to the demands of intimacy as a disciple of Christ. God makes very clear He desires to be the Lord of our life. What does that mean and how does it affect our daily life?

First, *we are to accept and adhere to Truth.* A. W. Tozer wrote a concise meaning of what Truth is: "Truth is a glorious but hard taskmaster. It makes moral demands upon us. It claims the sovereign right to control us. Truth will never stoop to be a servant but requires that all men serve it. It never flatters men and never compromises with them. It demands all or nothing and refuses to be used or patronized. It will be all in all or it will withdraw into silence."

The truth, principles and precepts of God are the foundation and building blocks for us to *"know and be led by Him"* in all of our life. To passively ignore the demands He has given for an intimate relationship with Him is to live within the boundaries of our own self-centeredness. It is imperative that we *read* His Word, *apply* its Truth and *appropriate* its promises.

Second, *truth is transparent, profound, sincere and factual.* When these virtues embrace our life, integrity and depth of character will be evident. There is no pretense or hypocrisy. Its demands necessitate our commitment and devotion to His Lordship. This is not a "one-and-done" vow, but a daily surrender to His control of every phase of our life. It is a *"becoming process"* where He is Lord of All. We walk daily in the reality of our faith, firmly fixed in Christ.

Third, *we can never attain what only Christ can give.* To plunder in the way of our selfish-independence is sure defeat. Surrender to His Lordship and Authority will embrace His awesome triumph. Our life becomes eternally effective when the Holy Spirit fills our personality with the adequacy of Christ. He is our mighty God for every need and our sufficiency for every endeavor. A radical change takes place and *we begin to mature in Christ and His life progressively lives through us.*

Fourth, *our spiritual vision focuses on the Infinite Greatness of God.* When David meditated on Almighty God, he was lost in the wonder of it all. He wrote, *"Great is the Lord and greatly to be praised, and His greatness is unsearchable (unfathomable, beyond our understanding)"* (Ps. 145:3). We are prompted by the Holy Spirit to unwavering faith in His plan, purpose and will for our life. Our life finds significance when embraced by steadfast believing faith. When our faith is focused on the Majesty of God ... everything else loses its finite significance. He fills our life with *"the fruit of the Spirit"* (Gal. 5:22) in an overflowing measure.

Fifth, *when we surrender to His Lordship, we can hear Him say, "Fear not, for I have redeemed you, I have called you by your name, you are mine"* (Isa. 43:1). Could there be any greater relationship than to hear Him say, **"You Are Mine"**? *"Whereby are given unto us exceeding great and precious promises: that by these we might be partakers of the divine nature"* (2 Peter 1:4). Surrendering to His Lordship and Authority will take us to an exciting life-filling venture with God as we walk daily in the consciousness of His Presence. We will experience the reality of resolute faith in the Lord of lords and King of kings where Christ reigns supreme on the throne of our heart. How blessed!

A Victorious Spiritual Life

How refreshing and challenging to see a Believer whose life radiates with the love of God. They "stand tall" above the many who are overcome with a self-oriented life focused on everything but God. Why is that so prevalent among many Believers? I think its because *His promises are not believed and their fulfillment is not expected.* A focused, experimental faith does not close its eyes to the purpose and will of God that lives beyond them.

These following words are very simple but profound when applied without reservation to our lives. They are a challenge if we are to engage them in the task of our spiritual journey: *"A victorious life finds reality ... by a life **surrendered to God** ... a life **controlled by God** ... and a life **lived for God**."* How inclusive this is but how few find this the criteria of their life.

What does it mean to live in the reality of a life *surrendered to God?* I will never forget the fateful day when Emperor Hirohito of Japan, with his highest commanding officers, met General MacArthur on the battleship Missouri. It signaled our victory over Japan at the cost of thousands of brave, courageous men. But the *term of surrender* is what stands foremost in this meeting. There was only one term used to underlie this surrender. It was to be **Unconditional!** *There was no debate, exception or immunity ... no terms, consideration, or deliberation: it was Unconditional!*

So it must be when we surrender our heart, will, and life to His Lordship and Authority. We surrender on His terms, not ours, which are **unconditional.** *A victorious life is initiated by a life surren-*

dered to God. Such a surrendered life opens the door for the Holy Spirit to have full and free access to all of our life. If God is to be in control, there must not be any impediments in our life that hinder His will, plan, and purpose for us. He will not impose Himself or His will on our self-independent life.

It is imperative that our attitude and motives be under His divine control. <u>Self</u>, with all of its entanglements and frustrations, must be surrendered to His authority. In the natural, we shun responsibility and being under His control. We want freedom, but ignore its demands. We want happiness, joy, and peace but seek it by indulging in the lusts of our carnal nature. This is unacceptable to God.

When God is in control of our life, He will redirect our self-imposed lifestyle and reveal unto us the futility and repulsiveness of our carnal nature. He will make clear to us the "path of life" (Ps. 16:11). We are made a new creation in Christ (2 Cor. 5:17). *A victorious life is controlled by God.*

We can now enjoy *a life lived for God.* Our attitudes and motives have made a radical change. We seek to please Him in our walk and in our life. We hunger and thirst for His Word, rejoice in the inconceivable privilege of coming into His Presence in prayer, and aspire to live in the reality of His presence and in the joy of our faith focused on Him each day. Wow!

What a blessing to live an exchanged life! See what a radical change has taken place. *The infinite love of God is the **subject** of our meditation, the **theme** of our praise, the **object** of our affections, the **joy** of our hearts, and the **consuming passion** of our life!* **We have found the Victorious Life by His Grace and seek to live it through His grace in His strength and His sufficiency!**

My Grace Or His Grace

We are so guilty of taking upon ourselves the concerns, the unknown and veiled issues of tomorrow. We dread what might be and seek to provide answers to what may never happen. Relying upon the futile resources of our finite and restricted abilities only festers the doubting heart that is fixed on <u>our grace</u> not <u>His Grace</u>.

He, whose name is the *"God of all Grace,"* will immeasurably exceed all the devastating circumstances that face His chosen ones. He will be found sufficient for each moment and each hour as they come. God has said, *"As thy days, so shall thy strength be"* (Deut. 33:25).

God does not bring us to the *"walls of Jericho"* without His victorious battle plan for victory. He did not lead the children of Israel to the bitter waters of Marah without providing the hidden branch. When Moses threw the hidden branch into the waters at God's command, they were made sweet and enabled them to have refreshing water to drink.

God proportions His Grace to the nature and season of trial, and gives the appropriate strength and support to meet that need. Oswald Chambers wrote, *"God does not give us grace for tomorrow, but grace for the moment."* His present grace is enough for the present necessity. We do not honor Him by anticipating trials, but by **confiding in His Faithfulness:** *"There has no temptation come upon you that is not common to man:* **But God is Faithful***, who will not suffer you to be tempted above that you are able to bear; but will with the temptation (trial, adversity) also make a way of escape that you will be able to bear it"*

(1 Cor. 10:13). *"Yea, though I walk through the valley of the shadow of death: I will fear no evil, for Thou art with me ..."* (Ps. 23:4). It is not <u>our grace</u> but <u>His Grace</u>. *"My Grace is Sufficient for thee."*

We so often brood, become discouraged and anxious when such response is not in God's plan for us. He does not want us to be overcome with the heavy issues of tomorrow, burdened down with all of its uncertainties and be subject to Satan's insidious ways to defeat us. He stands ever before us with His all-sufficient grace and says, *"Come unto me, all you that labor and are heavy laden, and I will give you rest. Take my yoke upon you, and learn of me; for I am meek and lowly in heart: and you shall find rest unto your souls. For my yoke is easy and my burden is light"* (Matt. 11:28-30).

We are insufficient for any trial or adversity, but **"our sufficiency is in God."** When tomorrow comes with its trials, Jesus will come with our tomorrow and with its trials too. Trust Him in all things! Let Him rule and reign in your heart.

When God told Abraham to take his son and offer him for a burnt offering upon one of the mountains, which I will tell thee of, he obeyed. On the third day he was asked by Isaac his son, *"Behold the fire and the wood: but where is the lamb for the burnt offering? And Abraham said,* **My son, God will provide** *himself a lamb for the burnt offering"* (Gen. 22: 2-8). When God stopped Abraham as he raised his knife to slay his son, God provided a ram in the thicket. Abraham named the place **"Jehovah-Jireh, the Lord will provide."**

What is your burden today? **"Cast all your care upon him;** *for He cares for you"* (2 Peter 5:7. **Surrender your will to His sovereign control ... and let God do in and through you what you cannot do.**

Lonely? ... You Are Not Alone!

I'm sure we have all gone through this frightening experience when, seemingly, our closest friends and loved ones are distant, insensitive, and unresponsive as we feel the cold binding reality of being <u>alone</u>. We are depressed and distraught amid the wreck of earthly joys and security, not knowing to whom or to what we should turn. Here is a message unto you from God: *"Never will I leave you. Never will I forsake you"* (Heb. 13:5).

Here is an ever true, unvarying, constant Friend. He is the Faithful One who is the same yesterday, today, and forever. The *unchangeableness of God!* What an anchor for the storm-tossed lonely soul. We have but to lift our heart in believing faith, and He will be our surety, our refuge and our strong tower from the taunting infiltration of Satan that has caused this devastating loneliness. *"For thou, O Lord, art a God full of compassion, and gracious, longsuffering, and plenteous in mercy and truth"* (Ps. 86:15).

Loneliness finds our focus upon the insecure, unstable foundation of our futile resources and strength. Those things we have held to for so long are like airy bubbles on the waters of a stream: we touch them and they are gone. The prop upon which for a lifetime we have been leaning, fails, and we now feel ourselves at the mercy of the pitiless storm ... ALONE! There is nothing abiding or secure amidst these fleeting shadows of our past.

BUT GOD! How blessed! The world has changed, but He to this moment changes not. He is without any variableness or shadow of turning. Follow Him through His pilgrimage here on earth:

the lame came to Him and were healed ... the blind received their sight ... the penitent He sent away forgiven ... all manner of human need HE met with His healing balm. Though ascended to the right hand of the Father, He is this same Jesus who has promised *"to do exceeding abundantly above all we can ask or think, according to His power that works in us"* (Eph. 3:20).

Your experience may be that of Paul: chained in a cold damp Roman prison when he felt that all had forsaken him, he said, *"Nevertheless, the Lord stood with me and strengthened me"* (2 Tim. 4:16-17). God compensates more than any earthly loss. The reality of His presence will enable us to be *rise victoriously above our circumstances while yet in them.* Through all the adversities, abuse, and persecution Paul endured, his testimony was, *"Now thanks be unto God, which **always causes us to triumph in Christ** ... we are unto God a sweet smelling savor of Christ, in them that are saved, and in them that perish"* (2 Cor. 2:14-15).

When told I had prostate cancer, God gave me the consoling comfort of His presence and power with these verses: *"Unless the Lord had been my help, I would have soon dwelt in silence. When I said, My foot is slipping, Your mercy and loving kindness, O Lord, held me up. In the multitude of my anxious thoughts within me, Your comforts cheer and delight my soul"* (Ps. 94:17-19).

Lonely? Not when He encompasses our life and our faith is steadfastly fixed on HIM. *"Fear thou not; for I am with you: be not dismayed, for I am your God: I will strengthen you; yea, I will help you; yea, I will uphold you with the right hand of my righteousness"* (Isa. 41:10).

Sovereignty

Years ago I was talking to a very godly man who had been through much turmoil and storms of life. His silver grey hair and his face, lined with grace, testified to the battles fought and victories won. I tried to look beneath those outward signs of conflict that defined his life, to the inner heart and will where *Christ enthroned his life.*

After numerous words of wise counsel, he said, *"No rainbow of Promise in the 'dark and cloudy sky' shines more radiantly than this:* **'The Lord Reigneth'** (Ps. 93:1). *God orders all events and overrules all for our good. Above every dark threatening cloud is the Silver Lining of His Presence and Power. It is He who* <u>brings</u> *the cloud, who brings us into it, and in mercy leads us through it."* Those words have been engraved on my heart the past sixty-six years.

Coupled with God's Sovereignty, he expounded on the truth that, *"We know that all things work together for good to them that love God ..."* (Rom. 8:28). How often I have meditated on this verse as my cherished goals were smitten and devastating circumstances seemed to consume me. The threatening clouds darkened the sky of my hope. But as I read further in vs. 29, I saw the silver lining of His Plan and Purpose: *"For whom he did foreknow, he also did predestinate* **to be conformed to the image of his Son ..."**

Accident, chance, luck, fate, destiny have no place in the Christian's creed. These are words expressed by a life without eternal meaning, without hope, and whose life has no firm foundation to anchor them in the storms of life. They are tossed to and fro by the meaningless shallow influences of a godless society whose premise is the glorifying of man at the expense of his eternal life.

The unbeliever is governed by his deceitful heart and seeks to justify himself within the boundaries of his finite perspective. They look from eyes blinded by Satan, not from *eyes renewed by the Holy Spirit*. They draw conclusions from a fallen sinful nature, not from *a recreated heart by God*. Their evaluations are limited to their carnal reactions, not by one whose *life is controlled by His Sovereign Power*.

How different it is for the Christian. We are not left to aimlessly drift at the mercy of treacherous waters. We are no <u>unpiloted vessel</u> without the sure direction and care of our Compassionate Lord. God stands with His loving arms around us to give our life purpose and eternal significance, led in His will and plan for our life.

David found the reality of God's Sovereignty as he faced the sustained pursuit of jealous Saul and his army who sought to kill him. He testifies in this <u>arena of horror</u>, "The Lord is my rock, and my fortress, and my deliverer; my God, my strength, in whom I will trust; my buckler, and the horn of my salvation, and my high tower" (Ps. 18: 2). His times were in the Hands of God, as even we who unwaveringly trust Him.

Subject to God's Sovereign control, our faith is not some dreamy contemplation or abstract speculation. It is one of pursuing with purpose, persevering with determination, dedicated to His leading, and progressively submissive to be *"conformed to the image of His Son"* (Rom. 8:29). How blessed is the transforming change we experience when Almighty God is the *Sovereign Authority of our heart and life*. We are unshackled from the most binding and wretched sin, released from anxiety and needless worry as *He brings us to a blessed freedom, peace and hope only He can give!*

May His Word be the foundation of our confidence, the surety of our consolation and the sufficiency of our every need as He reigns, the Authority and Sovereign of our life.

The Eternal Fountainhead

From whence do the *eternal life-giving waters* find their source of supply? Is it not from the *Fountainhead of Life, God Himself*? It is God that has created and provided for us this eternal flow of life-giving water from the <u>*fountainhead of His love, mercy and grace*</u> that sustains our thirsty soul.

As a boy, I was challenged with three friends to find the source of a mountain stream that flowed with refreshing clear water. We followed the stream at great length, seeking from whence it began. Finally, after hours of trekking through bush and barrier, we discovered the stream flowed freely from the stillness of a spring, which emanated from deep springs of water far below the surface that had a ceaseless supply. It was the *<u>fountainhead</u>*, the origin from which the stream of bubbling waters begun. Meandering its way to the valley below and beyond, it was the source of blessing to whoever would partake of it.

"He leadeth me beside the still waters" (Ps. 23:2). What a change from the surging tumultuous waters that convey the chaotic and confused character of man's bewildered mind. God comes to such and leads him to the quiet still waters of His presence and says, *"Be still and know that I am God"* (Ps. 46:10). Only as we open our hearts to His still small voice can we <u>*know Him*</u> in a measure of His infinite love to *"lead us in the paths of righteousness for His Name's sake"* (Ps. 23:3).

So we can be: **Free** from the confusion and frustration of misplaced faith. **Free** from distorted influences and superficial concepts of a satanic-controlled world. **Free** from the bondage of self-independence, greed, pride, and the vast encumbering chords that entangle our lives and distract our focus upon Him. **Free now**, to focus our eyes on the One who said, *"The young lions do lack, and suffer hunger: but they that seek the Lord shall not want any good thing"* (Ps. 34:10).

It is in the <u>secret of his presence</u> that we find His comfort and consolation, solace and support, mercy and grace, and the blessed leading of His Spirit. However simple or complex the problem of the moment may be, we are to ask for His guidance. We cannot *presume to know* what to do, only to fail ingloriously as Israel when they were grievously deceived by the Gibeonites (see Joshua 9:14). He will not always lead as in times past. Our spiritual receptivity to His leading will alert us to what the obedient heart has been told. Going forward in God's way and in God's time, we will know God's victory for us.

This is the experience of one who has found the *life-giving waters* of the <u>Fountainhead</u>. Jesus said, *"He who believes in me, as the Scripture said, from his innermost being shall flow rivers of living water"* (John 7:38). We will hear Him say, *"Commit thy way unto the Lord; trust also in Him; and He shall bring it to pass"* (Ps. 37:5).

"The secret of guidance is:

Committal-*the act of finality that lets go and lets God have His way.*

Confidence-*the attitude of implicit trust that leaves all our requests in His hands.*

Conclusion-*the divine action that brings God's will to pass in His own time and way, for His glory and our highest good"* (Dr. V. Raymond Edman).

"I sought the Lord and He heard me, and delivered me from all my fears" (Ps. 34:4). **Dare to Believe and trust Him.**

The Set Of The Sail

I never realized the intricacies and demanding attention that is needed and is so involved in sailing until I discussed *sailing* with my son-in-law. He loves to sail and enjoys the competition of a sailing race. We discussed many things, but the thing that intrigued me most was how the *"set of the sail"* which must respond to many weather conditions, waves, currents, and maneuvers that will decide whether it will win the race.

It is the *"set of the sail"* that determines its speed, direction, and complete control of the boat with the help of the helmsmen. Oftentimes a race is won or lost by the ability, skill, and experience of the man or men who are assigned to adjust the sail for various encounters.

This was so evident in the recent *"America's Cup"* races in San Francisco, where the ORACLE TEAM USA dramatically won the cherished "Cup." Reviewing the race, you cannot help but be immensely impressed with the Skipper, tactician, helmsmen, and the committed men working furiously with the *"set of the sail."* These are not ordinary weekend sailors but men with years of experience and training. They are dedicated to a goal to give every bit of themselves to maximize the results of their sailing craft. ORACLE TEAM USA was hailed as the greatest comeback victory in the 34 years of the *"America's Cup."*

As I thought through the particulars of the sailing craft, the men, and the tactics of the race, I thought how meaningful it is for each of us to be so dedicated to how we run the *"race of life"* that we are in. Every phase of our life needs to be under the authority and leadership of our Master Skipper, Jesus Christ. He is the One who initiates the decisions, determines our direction, and orchestrates our *"race of life."* He seeks to direct our life to be unreservedly committed and extend every effort to be victorious. The sail is an interesting part of the craft. It's made of special material to be strong, to interact perfectly to the sailors control, and properly respond to the winds and propel the craft as accurately and swiftly as possible. The sailors respond to the tactician who responds to the Skipper. Every part of the craft is built to interact with the teamwork of the crew. It is a masterful unit that works for one goal ... to Win!

Paul said, *"Do you not know that in a race all the runners race, but only one gets the prize ... Every athlete who goes into training conducts himself temperately and restricts himself in all things ... therefore I do not run uncertainly, without definite aim, but I buffet my body, handle it roughly, discipline it with hardships, and subdue it ... for fear of being rejected"* (Cor. 9:24-27) (Amp.Ver.).

So should we exemplify Paul and the rugged skilled sailors who *counted the cost and paid the price to win with ORACLE TEAM USA.*

I wonder if we have dedicated ourselves as they, to win the *"race of life"*? God has made us new creatures in Christ (supplied the craft) and set the race before us. It is for us to surrender every phase of our life to His sovereign control, to run without compromise of effort or principle, and that His commands will be followed in obedience. The Holy Spirit will so enable us to adjust to every encounter we face, supply the needed grace, purpose and perseverance, and ability to be *"more than a conqueror through Him that loved us"* (Rom. 8:29).

It all depends on the *"set of the sail."* When the *sail is set under His control* there is nothing short but glorious victory!

He Knoweth

How wonderful it is to have the assurance and confidence of knowing the way we are to pursue. We go forward with a triumphant attitude and buoyant certainty that the decisions we have made will be productive to our benefit, and the way we are taking is the right way. However, we are often persuaded by a selfish attitude, a misdirected faith, or unknowingly influenced by unwise counsel. Feelings can be deceptive when darkness seems to engulf our very being. Dangers become imaginary or greatly exaggerated, and doubt and uncertainty loom unawares. Awakened to this dilemma, we become distressed and distraught and lift up our hearts in despair and sigh as Job, *"O that I knew where I might find Him!"* (Job 23:3).

"He Knoweth the Way!" Why do we go through so much anxiety and stress when He stands ready *"to lead me in the paths of righteousness for His Name's sake"*? (Ps. 23:3). God gives us a clear and concise revelation of His leading: *"Ask, and it shall be given you; seek, and you shall find; knock, and it shall be opened unto you: for every one that asketh receiveth; and he that seeketh findeth; and to him that knocketh it shall be opened"* (Matt. 7:7-8).

God knows the boundaries of our bewilderment. He understands the sigh of our heart, the distress of our soul and the searching for His leading to know His will and way. In faith we declare, however faintly, *"Lord, I believe; help thou my unbelief"* (Mark 9:24). It is then that faith takes over ... our sighing becomes a song, our weakness His strength, our distress His peace, and the deceiving darkness exchanged for the Light of His Presence and Power. We have dared to believe and trust Him fully. Without reservation, we *"cast all of our care on Him for He cares for us"* (1 Peter 5:7).

BUT GOD! These two words can make all the difference in the world. Unreservedly, we lift up our hearts in childlike faith and proclaim to God as Job, ***"But He knoweth the way** that I take: when He hath tried me, I shall come forth as gold"* (Job 23:10). With unwavering trust in the Faithful One, we must learn to discount darkness and its deceit, the infiltrating ways of Satan to discourage and defeat, and the pressure of an ungodly world, for ***"He Knoweth the Way."***

Read the words of Dr. V. Raymond Edman, past President and Chancellor of Wheaton College: *"Our asking must be made in the fixed attitude of faith. Faith is not fanaticism or fervor, which we foment for ourselves. Faith in God is a quiet confidence that He hears our prayers and answers in His own way and time. Faith is counting on God and not anything in ourselves. Faith is to be unwavering, unshaken, undisturbed persuasion that God's will is being done. Any divided mindedness on our part destroys our receptivity to the answer God has for us. No time is wasted when we pause to pray nor are we delayed because we wait upon God when the way is dangerous or dark. To wait upon God, no time is lost."* Plant your faith in the certainty of God's care for you!

God is never too late nor does He ever come with too little. True prayer, believing faith, obedience and faithful waiting on the Lord are essential to hearing God say, *"This is the way, walk you in it"* (Isaiah 30:21). *"The hand of the Lord is upon all them for good ... that seek Him"* (Ezra 8:22). ***"He Knoweth the Way that I shall take"*** (Job 23:3). In perseverance and patience, faith and trust, dedication and determination ... let us surrender to His leading and follow Him fully. May we be sensitive to the Holy Spirit who will faithfully direct our steps. Dare to believe and trust Him fully. He is Faithful that promised and will care for you.

They That Wait

I don't know of anybody that takes pleasure in waiting regardless of what the occasion may be. It is a demanding and often frustrating experience. We get anxious, irritable and cantankerous. It takes an exercise of patience and perseverance to simply _wait_ when our button is on "fast forward."

To the Believer, God has said, *"They that wait upon the Lord shall renew their strength. They shall mount up with wings as eagles, shall run and not be weary and shall walk and not faint"* (Isa. 40:31). In your spiritual journey, have you ever had to _wait_ for His direction, His leading, His answer to the pressing need that seems must be answered NOW? We feel the stress of our human nature for immediate answers to the darkness of uncertainty and the insecurity of our resources to be met, not tomorrow, but NOW.

Such an attitude exemplifies our lack of resting in the Lord, placing our faith in His Sovereign control, and recognizing _we_ must "cast all your anxiety on Him" (1 Peter 5:7) and let God do what we cannot do. True and simple faith does not _hold on_ to the need but unreservedly commits it into His loving compassion and care. It is like mailing a letter. As long as we stand at the mailbox and hold onto our letter, it will never reach its destination. Not until we release it and commit it to the mailbox will the postman retrieve it and send it to the desired address. We must trust the Postal Service to do its job. This, we must do when we dare to trust God. *"Commit thy way unto the Lord; trust also in Him; and He shall bring it to pass"* (Ps. 37:5). What are the **key** words in this verse? They are _commit_ and _trus_t. In whom or in what? THE LORD.

We place great emphasis on God's Word but so often fail to appropriate its irrevocable promises to us. God simply says, if we will commit our need <u>unto Him</u> and dare to <u>*trust Him fully,*</u> that He will bring it to pass! This same promise is made more emphatically in Prov. 3:5-6. Read the Amplified version for better clarity: *"Lean on, trust and be confident in the Lord with all of your heart and mind, and do not rely on your own insight or understanding. In all your ways know, recognize and acknowledge Him, and He will direct and make plain your paths."*

Frustration, anxiety and self-imposed stress bring us into a state of doubt and unbelief. These characteristics are not a part of the Believer whose faith is wholly in the Lord. God gives unto the trusting Believer His grace to wait patiently on the Lord. God says, *"But those who wait for the Lord – who expect, look for and hope in Him – shall change and renew their strength and power ..."* (Isa. 40:31).

We so often exchange <u>*waiting on the Lord*</u> by imposing **<u>our input</u>** of trying to do God's promise **<u>our way</u>**. God can only make real His promise when we <u>*obediently*</u> follow the conditions of His promise to us: *"Therefore will the Lord wait, that He may be gracious unto you, and therefore will He be exalted, that He may have mercy upon you: for the Lord is a God of judgment: blessed are all they that wait for Him"* (Isa. 30: 18). And what will He do? *"Behold I will do a new thing; now it shall spring forth; shall you not know it? I will even make a way in the wilderness, and rivers in the desert"* (Isa. 43:19).

Claim His promises: *"they shall mount up with wings as eagles; they shall run, and not be weary; and they shall walk, and not faint."* (Isa. 40:31) Waiting upon God is not wasted time, but time invested in His care and Sovereign control for our good and His glory.

This Is The Victory

Whenever we are engaged in any distressful situation, we are often frustrated in knowing what to do, or in whom we should trust for wisdom and direction. We plod through dreary days and sleepless nights looking for the answer to our dreadful need. John said, *"this is the victory that overcometh the world, **even our faith**"* (1 John 5:4).

What is this *faith* that overcomes the world and all of the encounters we are called to face? Why is it such a vital part of our spiritual journey? What happens when we exercise true faith?

Faith is placing unwavering confidence in God: that He hears our prayers and answers in His own way and time. It is placing undivided, resolute persuasion that God will bring *"me up also out of the miry clay and set my feet upon a rock, and establish my goings ... and put a new song in my mouth, even praise unto our God: many shall see it, and fear, and shall trust in the Lord" Ps. 40:2-3.* It is relying completely on the validity of God and His Word, not anything in our selves.

The amplified version makes very clear the essence of faith: *"Now faith is the assurance (the confirmation, the title-deed) of things (we) hope for, being the proof of things (we) do not see and the conviction of their reality ... faith perceiving as real fact what is not revealed to the senses"* (Heb. 11:1).

Faith is a vital part of every phase of our life. True full-functioning faith is the mainspring of every spiritual achievement. It is the effective action of the solution of all our problems, in every single thing, small or great, in the home or at play, in our business or at leisure ... in everything that affects the Believer's life.

As you read Hebrews 11, you will find that _faith_ was the dynamic of all Believers did. Every phase of their life was based on a steadfast faith in God ... Who was able, willing and powerful enough to subdue every encounter and put to naught the evil forces arrayed against them, even Satan himself. Faith embraced all their actions and attitudes. This chapter exemplifies men and women whose entire being was solidified and motivated by faith in their supernatural all-powerful, faithful God!

What are the results of fully functioning faith? It is the mighty working of God in and through us, achieving things beyond our ability. It results in HIS LIFE living in and through us to manifest His plan and purpose for our lives. The whole eleventh chapter of Hebrews lists, in a measure, the faith that was active in Christians who dared to believe and would not recant their faith even when it cost their life.

Such faith, in all of its aspects, is seen in the writings of all four Apostles, Paul, Peter, John and James: the faith that *saves*, in Romans; the faith that *frees*, in Galatians; the faith that is *tested*, in Peter; the faith that *overcomes*, in John; the faith that *works*, in James; the faith that *endures and achieves*, in Hebrews; the faith that *sanctifies*, in Thessalonians; the faith that *is fought for*, in Timothy; the faith that *centers in Christ*, in Ephesians and Colossians.

"Therefore, since we are surrounded by such a great cloud of witnesses, let us throw off everything that hinders and the sin that so easily entangles, and let us run with perseverance the race marked out for us. **Let us fix our eyes on Jesus**, *the author and perfecter of our faith"* (Heb. 12:1-2). **"This is the victory that overcometh the world, even our faith"** (1 John 1:4).

His Way

Distressing concerns and unsettling situations that interrupt our spiritual journey constantly confront us. Disturbing sounds of meaningless distractions challenge us mentally and emotionally. Doubt, fear, and unrest attack our faith and cause us to reason within ourselves. Cunningly, Satan seeks to take advantage of our dilemma and cause discouragement, dismay and defeat.

"Surely the arm of the Lord is not too short to save, nor his ear too dull to hear" (Isa. 59: 1). And again, *"fear was on every side ... But I trusted in Thee, O Lord: I said, Thou art my God.* ***My times are in thy hand ...****"* (Ps. 31: 13-15).

We have a choice in such times as to whom we will trust. Shall we trust <u>our</u> vacillating and faulty resources, or shall we *dare to trust God* to lift us out of the dilemma of our distress and meet our need according to His plan and purpose? To plunder in the way of selfish will and human judgment is sure defeat. To surrender to **<u>His Way</u>** and Authority leads to a glorious triumph in His time and in His way.

I love the profound truth of the words we often sing but all too often we do not take to heart and embrace in believing faith: *"Be still my soul! The Lord is on thy side; Bear patiently the cross of grief or pain. Leave to thy God to order and provide; In every change He faithful will remain. Be still my soul! thy best, thy Heavenly Friend through thorny ways leads to a joyful end"* (Katharina A. von Schlegel).

What is the key? To *be still* and hear Him say, *"Fear not; (there is nothing to fear)* **for I am with you;** *do not look around you in terror and be dismayed,* **for I am your God. I will strengthen and harden you (to difficulties);** *yes,* **I will help you;** *yes,* **I will uphold you and retain you** *with my righteous right hand of righteousness and justice"* (Isaiah 41: 10). How blessed to simply **release completely** all of our anxieties into His Hands and **trust Him fully** to work out His will in the devastating circumstances we encounter.

A simple truth is revealed in the words of the hymn, "*God Will Make a Way.*" May it express the confidence we have in Him: "*God will make a way where there seems to be no way. He works in ways we cannot see; He will make a way for me. He will be my guide, hold me closely to his side. With love and strength for each new day; He will make a way, He will make a way for me*" (Donald J. Moen).

Is there any better way than **trusting Him without reservation?** He said, **"Delight thyself** *also in the Lord; and He shall give you the desires of your heart. ...* **Commit thy way** *unto the Lord;* **trust also in Him;** *and He shall bring it to pass"* (Ps. 37: 5, 7).

Doubt, fear, anxiety, apprehension, worry, uncertainty, distrust, and a mindset of other negative thoughts are not in God's plan for our life. He has given us His irrevocable promises based upon the faithfulness and power of His Word and the greatness of His Majesty. (2 Peter 1:4)

We need to recognize our inability in the light of His all-sufficiency ... turn our tunnel-vision faith and focus our eyes to new horizons God will give to us when we "Dare to Believe." We need to turn from self-imposed walls of devastating bondage that restrict and bind us and let God enlarge the boundaries of our life with His Presence and Power.   We need to cast ourselves with all of our finite limitations, with unwavering faith on the greatness of His Power and the Sufficiency of His Grace. This is HIS way!

True Friendship

The measure of our relationship is proved in the reality of our commitment and dedication to another. Words are shallow and unconvincing when our actions prove questionable and unrealistic. We are very fortunate to have five or six *"true friends"* during our lifetime.

We can confide to such a friend our most intimate concerns and issues with resolute confidence. They share our victories and defeats, our heartaches and rejoicing, our loss and our gain. Regardless of what devastating encounters we face, they stand with steadfast faithfulness to honor their unspoken vow as a *"true friend."*

Such relationships are deeper than being a companion, acquaintance, comrade or ally. It goes to the core of our very being and acts as an anchor and an unmovable rock that secures our relationship with a bond of understanding, compassion and sincere love and concern. There is no superficial exterior that covers any hidden thoughts, mind-set or motives. There is complete transparency in all of their communication and attitude to the other.

True friendship is beautifully illustrated in the covenant between David and Jonathon. There was such a bond of friendship between them that it is extended even after Jonathon was killed in battle. David was concerned if there was anyone left of Saul's household.

"Ziba said unto the king, Jonathon has yet a son, which is lame on his feet." When Mephibosheth was brought to David, he said, *"Fear not: for I will surely show thee kindness for Jonathon thy father's sake, and*

will restore thee all the land of Saul thy father; and thou shall eat bread at my table continually" (2 Sam. 9:6-11).

This was *true friendship* that began with his bonded covenant with Jonathon. Mephebosheth was called into the King's presence and exalted, given a glorious inheritance because of the merits of Jonathon. Mephibosheth not only ate at the king's table continually, but also was considered as one of David's sons. Grace, mercy, and love flowed full and free from David to this exiled crippled son of Jonathon. Redeemed, reconciled, and restored to freedom, peace, and love, *because of another.*

Are we not reminded of God's infinite love to us? We are shown mercy and grace because of Another, Jesus Christ, the Son of God. Do we deserve His concern and compassion? Can we earn His bond of love and friendship? In no way!

"You hath He quicken, who were dead in trespasses and sins; wherein in times past we walked according to the course of this world, according to the prince of the power of the air, the spirit that now works in the children of disobedience ... But God, who is rich in mercy, for His great love wherewith He loved us, even when we were dead in sins, hath quickened us together in Christ, (by grace are you saved) and hath raised us up together to sit in heavenly places in Christ Jesus. For by grace are you saved through faith; and that not of yourselves: it is the gift of God: not of works that we should boast" (Eph. 2: 1-9).

True friendship is born in heaven, not only for our life here but bonded together by the infinite love of God through Jesus Christ for eternity. **"Greater love hath no man than this, that a man lay down his life for his friends. You are my friends if you do whatsoever I command you"** (John 15:13-14).

Contentment

It is amazing how many people are engrossed with being *discontent*. It seems that nothing brings the enjoyment and fulfillment their heart craves for. They can be secure financially, able to have a gracious measure of what they want, and still live in the anxiety of discontent. Why are they so discontented? Let's look at a few *"potholes"* that lead to such a negative critical life.

Self-centeredness is the cancer at the core of discontent. Life is built upon the foundation of *"What is there in it for me?"* Whatever the occasion, relationship or cause, they can only think of themselves and how they will be recognized, approved or accepted. It matters not if they are qualified, capable or competent ... their ego, self-image and self-esteem must be served. They must be seen as superior and authoritative. Anything short of this is unacceptable and intolerable. They become dissatisfied, upset and devastated ... *discontented*.

There's only one way ... My Way. Why is it so difficult to accept other people's opinion or decision rather than ours? Why do we always feel others should accept *our* way rather than being receptive to *their* way? Oftentimes we cannot see the forest for the trees. We are so engrossed with what *we* think or *the way something should be done* that we are completely oblivious to any other opinion. We will not bend to even hear what others have to say.

Such behavior is manifested because *we are apprehensive and fearful that we may be wrong. We are terrified by the thought of others thinking we are something we are not.* Therefore, we endeavor to intimidate others by our <u>self-proclaimed</u> superiority.

Insecurity. We feel insecure for a number of reasons. It's not because we do not have adequate finances ... it stems from things much deeper that affects our attitude, perception of life, and selfish desires. Our focus is not on the Lord, although we insincerely pretend that it is. Our focus is not on helping others, although we make an effort to do something special for someone. We get self-gratification from such actions that stems from our selfish motivations.

Living in self-denial is a constant companion. We are reluctant to face the reality of our problem. We excuse our concerns on others or simply deny they exist. We refuse to listen to others by denying that our problem has seriously affected our behavior. We turn, rather, to things that will give us temporary satisfaction and inflate our ego. We thrive on what <u>we</u> have done, who <u>we</u> are and dismiss any consideration of others. As a result, *we live a suppressed, discontented, and unfulfilled life.*

What is the answer? We must look within and *acknowledge truthfully whom we are.* Address our need in the light of God's Word and let Him make us what He wants us to be. What we believe will affect how we live. *Make God's Word the <u>standard</u> that governs our life.* Contentment does not depend on who we are or what we have: it depends on *Whom our eyes are fixed upon and in Whom we put our faith in.* Paul said, **"Fix your eyes on Jesus, the Author and Finisher of our faith"** (Heb. 12:2).

When Christ is the <u>*priority of our life*</u> ... the <u>*focus of our desires*</u> ... and the <u>*joy of our heart*</u> ... there is no room for the critical, self-inflicted ways of discontent. *He becomes the Source of our strength and conquering Spirit that enables us to live courageously and triumphantly.* Paul said, **"I have learned that in whatsoever state I am, therewith to be content"** (Phil. 4:10).

Our Choice

How devastating it is when the results of something of <u>our choice</u> turns out completely different than what we envisioned. Oftentimes, <u>our choice</u> was not given thorough consideration, was motivated by our emotions, or we followed unsound advice. The consequences can be of little consequence or they can be devastating. In either case, **it is imperative that <u>our choices</u> are of God's leading, not ours.**

I'm sure you have heard the phrase, *"The grass is not always greener on the other side."* Many attractions can be a subtle illusion rather than reality. Even making a <u>choice</u> when things look stable, secure and inviting, they can be to our detriment. It is important for us to be discerning, wise, and judicious *as we seek the Lord in all things.*

Abraham and Lot's cattle had multiplied exceedingly. The servants were angry and discontented with each other. It was necessary for them to divide the land and each have their own territory to raise their livestock. Abraham graciously gave Lot the opportunity to *choose* which part of the land he desired. Although Abraham had the right to whatever land he wanted, he gave Lot first choice. (Gen. 13:9-18)

A desirable opportunity does not always mean it will guarantee success, fulfillment, or it's God's will for us. It is of primary importance to seek His leading, pray for His interceding, wait for His assurance, and hear Him say, *"This is the way, walk you in it"* (Isa. 30:21). We must evaluate our own abilities, experience, and skills relating to how we will respond and handle the responsibilities we will face. Our character, emotions, and knowledge are important virtues in making _our choice_. It will reveal the reality of our faith and our intimate walk and relationship with the Lord.

First, Abraham was a man of faith and sought to be led and embraced by God in every phase of his life. **Abraham left his choice in God's Hand!** He had no doubt that if he was left with the most desolate and undesirable land, that God would intercede in such a way that it would bring glory to His Name and good to Abraham. What happened?

Lot surveyed the land. He saw the well-watered plains of Jordon. His selfish carnal spirit envisioned ultimate affluence and immeasurable wealth to have such rich green pastures to raise his livestock. He would have extensive influence and power. He was motivated by the *"lust of the eye, the lust of the flesh and the pride of life"* (1 John 2:16).

Are these not the temptations that prompt many of _our choices_? He took great pride in choosing the best of the land, but his choice was undermined not only by his lusts and pride but by the *well-watered plains of Jordon and the sin that prevailed without restraint in Sodom and Gomorrah. They were his downfall*. **He did not seek God or seemingly care that God was not in the equation of his choice.**

How penetrating this important occurrence should be to us. What happens when we face superb opportunities? Do we seek His will, discernment, wisdom and direction? Is the Lord our primary consideration in making _our choice_? We are often the culprits of many dreadful consequences when _our choice_ is motivated by our selfish pride and ego.

May His will be our choice and be the Preeminent One in all our decisions, *as we walk in His companionship each day. Dare to Believe and Trust Him with unwavering faith.*

> **"Trust in the Lord with all your heart and lean not unto your own understanding. In all your ways acknowledge Him, and He will direct your path"** (Pro. 3:5-6).

Appropriate And Apply... Receive And Rejoice

Four words that can be a revolution in your everyday life. How fitting these words are to Christians in relation to their spiritual journey. Yet, how often we find so many who ignore or fail to take into account the profound affect they can have in their life. Are you one of those who are not being impacted by their power?

When a Believer reads God's Word and is confronted with God's irrevocable promises and simply concludes, "That is so *appropriate* to my situation," I wonder what further reaction they have? When they fail to *own its truth or make it a reality in their life,* they *lose the purpose* for which it was intended.

What does this amazing word ***appropriate*** mean? It means suitable, proper, fitting and correct. If what we read is applicable to our situation ... why do we bypass the opportunity to *lay hold* of its truth to empower our life and meet the need we are facing?

I think we are amiss when we admit the relevance and significance of His Word but fail so miserably to ***apply*** its truth to our life. It's like being invited to a special occasion and seeing the sumptuous food beautifully displayed, and we say, *"How appropriate"* but fail to partake of its satisfying nourishing qualities. **We need to *apply* what we read, make it our own** and **relevant to our life.** It will intensify our faith, challenge our commitment, and deepen our intimate relationship with Christ.

Consider another situation that so often occurs. God has given to us many promises but we are not willing to ***receive*** them as His gift.

We think it is necessary for us to <u>work for the gift</u> or make ourselves <u>acceptable, worthy or approved</u> to receive the grace in which it is given. Our salvation is the *"gift of God."* We receive it by faith. It is not a reward, obligation or compensation. *God's Grace is giving us what we do not deserve.* By His Grace He has exercised mercy in withholding the wrath we deserve. However glorious this is, we must by faith *accept and receive* what He provided to us. **The significance of the gift is realized only when we receive and accept it.**

When we *take delivery of* (accept and receive) what He alone has provided to us by His Grace, "We *rejoice* with joy unspeakable and full of glory" (1 Peter 1:8). We glory in the magnitude of His grace and the manifestation of His love:

"His divine power hath given unto us all things *that pertain unto life and godliness, through the knowledge of Him that hath called us to glory and virtue: whereby are given unto us exceeding great and precious promises that by these* **we may be partakers of the divine nature"** (2 Peter 1: 3-4).

When you put these four words together, it describes the incredible opportunity every Believer has in Christ. When we <u>Appropriate and Apply</u> ... <u>Receive and Rejoice</u>, **we are bonded in an integral relationship with the Lord that exceeds our greatest expectations. We walk in 'newness of life' only He can give.** These are but a few of the irrevocable promises that we can make our walk with the Lord a reality in our life.

Let us not simply adhere to the truth but make His Truth, principles and precepts of His Word a *living part of our spiritual journey.* You'll never be the same. ***It will be the Life of Christ living in and through you for His glory. Appropriate and Apply ... Receive and Rejoice!***

Becoming

Many Christians today are not growing and maturing in their spiritual life. They are not being used of the Lord or being a blessing and encouragement to others. They attend church and other activities of the church but seem to be satisfied with their spiritual status. Peter admonishes us to *"grow in grace, and in knowledge of our Lord and Savior Jesus Christ"* (2 Peter 3:18).

When a Believer is not growing in their spiritual life, it is detrimental to their faith. Possibly, they may have never been taught or challenged to *"grow in grace."* Paul challenged young Timothy to *"study and be eager and do your utmost to present yourself to God approved (tested by trial), a workman who has no cause to be ashamed, correctly analyzing and accurately dividing – rightly handling and skillfully teaching – the Word of Truth"* (2 Tim. 2:15) (Amp. Ver.). What does it mean to *"grow in grace"*?

First, we must have a receptive spirit in response to the Holy Spirit that awakens us to our need to grow and mature in our faith. When we respond He will create within our hearts a *"hunger and thirst"* to have a deeper walk with the Lord.

Secondly, the Holy Spirit will *challenge us to read, meditate, and study God's Word, the Bible.* He will give us enlightenment, understanding, and spiritual discernment of what we read. His Word will become our *"daily bread"* and spiritual nourishment in implementing our growth. We will be encouraged, inspired and fed through the Scriptures.

Thirdly, *fellowship with other Believers and those mature in their spiritual life* will be a great asset to our study. They can be a spiritual mentor, counselor, and tutor in helping us grow in grace. They will also challenge us to a consistent sincere prayer life that will be a daily concern and integral part of our spiritual journey. *Our spiritual life will never be any greater than the time we spend in prayer.*

We do not instantly become an effective, fruitful and mature Believer when we first receive Jesus Christ as our Savior. It is the <u>*beginning*</u> of an exciting journey where Christ is our Lord and Authority. We will seek to adorn our life with the virtues of Christ and mature in our faith.

"Growing in grace" in our faith is a **becoming process.** The process will be applying ourselves to the study of His Word, important times of meditation, sincere daily prayer, and fellowship with other Believers as we take part in the ministry of the Gospel to others. Our spiritual life is not a stagnant "status quo" existence but an *exciting spiritual journey* that will develop into a steadfast faith, grounded in the Scriptures, and a blessing and encouragement to others.

We must persevere and develop strong and fervent spiritual behavior in this **becoming ... *"to be conformed (molded) into the image of His Son (and share inwardly His likeness)"*** (Rom. 8:29). It will radically transform your life; develop a new and exciting standard of living, and a life pleasing to the Lord and a blessing and inspiration to others.

I trust you will have a hunger and thirst to be like Jesus and used of Him to glorify His Name. It is a <u>*becoming process*</u> but one that will take you to a *life on the highest plane!*

Together We Can

We so often try to accomplish tasks that are too big for us, whether physically, mentally or emotionally. Sometimes the results are unwelcomed, unacceptable, failed, or to our detriment. Then, we ask ourselves, "Why didn't I get someone to help me?" How foolish were our actions and what a price to pay for not being more thoughtful.

I have a little reminder on my desk that shows three men holding up a platter with three round silver balls. The inscription of challenge reads, "Together We Can." It reminds me of how many times I try and do things in my own strength, mentality, and giftedness only to find discouragement and defeat. If only I would have asked someone to <u>help</u> me it would have been so easy.

I've often thought how this applies so real to our spiritual life. We have available to us God the Father, God the Son, and God the Holy Spirit. Three divine powers that invite us again and again to let *them* do what we in ourselves cannot do. Why do we shun such unbelievable reliable assistance?

One thing stands forcibly before us ... **stubbornness!** Why are we so stubborn? Well, I guess we all want to prove our worth and capability. *Who cares?* We don't have to prove ourselves to anybody ... we are what we are. We often defy what others see as a need in our life. Their warning or admonition goes unwelcomed. We are reluctant to accept counsel or advice from others. We are just *stubborn!*

Another issue is ... ***pride!*** We are reluctant to admit that the task may be more than we counted on. We cannot let others know that we are not capable to handle the encounter we face. So, we plunge forward in our inability, weakness, and indifference to conquer what is beyond our ability. We cannot stand for others to know there is anything we cannot confront with our giftedness. God's Word says, *"Pride goeth before destruction, and a haughty spirit before a fall"* (Prov. 16:18). Coupled with pride are haughtiness, self-exaltation, conceit, arrogance, and misplaced self-confidence. When these attitudes encompass our personality, we portray to others a defensive characteristic and an attitude to our own detriment.

When I was a Boy Scout I was taught how three cords were incredibly stronger than two. Entwined together they form a combined unified strength, capable of performing difficult tasks. In our spiritual journey, we need the strength of the Father, Son, and Holy Spirit. The daily tasks we often face are too overwhelming for us in our strength alone. We need to exercise faith that HE will be our strength, hope and power.

Paul said, *"My grace is sufficient for thee: for my strength is made perfect in weakness. Most gladly therefore will I rather glory in my infirmities, that the power of Christ may rest upon me. Therefore I take pleasure in my infirmities, in reproaches, in necessities, in persecutions, in distresses for Christ's sake: for when I am weak, then am I strong"* (2 Cor. 12:9-10).

Yet another promise from God, *"Fear thou not; for I am with you: be not dismayed; for I am your God: I will strengthen you; yea, I will help you, yea, I will uphold you with the right hand of my righteousness"* (Isa. 41:10).

"Together We Stand" ... *When we rely upon the divine three, the Father, Son, and the Holy Spirit to be our sufficiency for every task we face and every step we take it is a "win-win" situation for our good and His glory!*

A Beacon Of Light

Have you ever been in absolute darkness where you couldn't see anything? I remember when my wife and I visited Mammoth Cave in Kentucky. As we descended into the cave, we stood in a very large cavern. The guide said, "Now don't be afraid; I'm going to shut off the lights along our trail, and we will be in *absolute darkness."* When she did, the darkness was so intense that you felt as if it was penetrating your very being.

Momentarily, someone on the other side of the cavern lit a very small birthday candle, and the light from the small candle illuminated the vast cavern, and it came to life. I was absolutely amazed that the very small candle made such an unbelievable difference as it penetrated the darkness. It's not how much light _we have_ that makes a difference ... but rather ... *HIS LIGHT that shines forth in its saving grace.*

Jesus said, *"You are the light of the world. A city that is set on a hill cannot be hid"* (Matt. 5:14). It isn't anything within ourselves that causes us to be _light_ in a darkened sinful world. It is **His Life being lived through us.** John said, *"In Him was life; and the life was the light of men"* (John 1:4). However insignificant we think we are, by His power we can be as the _very small candle_ and light up the sinful darkness where we are, distill the penetrating satanic obscurity that engulfs so many ... and reveal unto them **The Light of the world, Jesus Christ.**

I have often been amazed at the effectiveness of a lighthouse strategically built where ships in distress can see its brilliant light. We have a lighthouse at the end of our peninsula, and through the years, it has been a *"guiding light"* for ships to know their location and steer away from lurking danger. The *lighthouse keeper* has the important responsibility to keep the brilliant lights and huge reflectors in exceptional condition. The lives of men and the destiny of ships depend upon his extraordinary care. When I heard of the responsibilities he must take, I thought of my own life in relation to being given spiritual responsibilities to reflect <u>His Light</u> through my life. *"For you were sometimes darkness, but now are you light in the Lord:* **walk as children of light** ... *proving what is acceptable to the Lord"* (Eph. 5:8,10).

As God's children we are responsible to live and walk as *"children of light."* We have eyes to see and ears to hear what the Spirit says unto us. May the cry of our heart be that of David who said, *"Create in me a clean heart, O God: and renew a right spirit within me"* (Ps. 51:10). God desires a *receptive heart and a responsive spirit* that adheres to His words, *"This is the way, walk you in it"* (Isa. 30:21). We can only *reflect the light* ... even as the moon and the trillions of stars reflect the brilliant light of the sun.

People's hearts and minds are blinded by Satan and the evil that consumes them. *"In whom the god of this world has blinded the minds of them that believe not, lest the light of the glorious gospel of Christ, who is the image of God, should shine unto them"* (2 Cor. 4:4). O that we may be clean through the Word and reflect the *"light of God"*... that through our words and walk, attitude and life we shall reflect His love, mercy, and grace.

God waits patiently for us to enter into the *"secret of His presence"* that He may reveal unto us the greatness of His grace and His infinite glory. O that He might *electrify our hearts* with His incomprehensible Majesty. Lost in the wonder of it all we will be a <u>reflector of His Light</u> and live in the might of His power for His glory.

My Radiology Report

Some people are afraid of medical tests, chemical profiles, blood analysis, and other medical examinations. I recently had a radiology report and was astounded by its findings. The test employs the use of imaging to both diagnose and treat disease visualized within the body. The imperfections inside our bodies are revealed and alert the doctor to take proper action to prevent future growth or damage by the disease to our bodies.

My radiology report was diagnosed as having a tumor on my liver. This required a procedure that inserted the proper medication to cut off the oxygen to the tumor and surrounding area and cause the cancer cells and tumor to die. A later MRI scan showed the tumor had *reduced considerably*. Medical treatment takes time to eradicate or cure a disease.

As I thought through all that was taking place, I was reminded that what we see on the outside does not always reveal the problem within our body that is causing all the trouble. Spiritually, many make a profession of being a Christian. They adhere to the Truth, take part in many of the ministries of the Church, but the Truth of redeeming grace has never penetrated their heart. They have never embraced the Truth that radically changes their life. Their faith is simply an <u>outward profession</u>, not from an <u>inward possession</u>.

It is much like my radiologist's report. Samuel looked for God's chosen one to be the king of Israel: *"The Lord said unto Samuel, Look not on his countenance or on the height of his statue; because I have refused him: for the Lord seeth not as man seeth; for* **man looketh on the outward appearance, but the Lord looketh on the heart"** (1 Sam. 18:7).

God sees the inner workings of our heart: the attitude and motives that are initiated from selfish-independence that seeks to gratify the deceitfulness of our heart. As the radiology report revealed the deficiencies that were within my body, so God sees not only an insincere profession of faith but also the motives that promote such selfish actions on our part. *"Keep thy heart with all diligence for out of it are the issues of life"* (Prov. 4:23). We can fool men, influence their minds and attract their interest ... but *we cannot fool God!*

God said, "The heart is deceitful above all things and desperately wicked: who can know it? I the Lord search the heart, I try the reins, even to give every man according to his ways, and according to the fruit of his doings" (Jer. 17: 9-10). God sees what is within our heart: the imperfections and sinful motivations that embrace our life. Our outward profession and appearance do not convince him.

Because of our pride, we do not want to face this enlightening reality. We take every precaution to make a good impression, appear what we wish we were, and endeavor to disguise our real self. What a foolish effort and choice when God says, Come as you are with all our shallow profession, insincere selfish projections, and let Me forgive your sin and make you a new creation in Christ. David questions, *"Lord who shall abide in thy tabernacle? Who shall dwell in thy holy hill? He that walked uprightly, and worked righteousness, and speak the truth in his heart"* (Ps. 15: 1-2).

The measure of God's Authority, His Sovereign control of our life ... is to the degree to which faith, hope, trust and dependence upon God is a realty in our life. Dare to believe and trust Him fully!

His Voice In The Wilderness

If you have ever hiked in faraway places, free from caustic noise, and scathing distractions, you can appreciate the splendor and peace of *penetrating quietness*. Whether it be in the luxuries of a sumptuous, beautiful woodland, the gracefulness of a mountain brook flowing through an alpine forest, or the distinctiveness of the quiet unsullied desert ... we seize the moment given to us by God to marvel and stand in awe of **His voice in the wilderness**.

So many miss this distinct privilege because they are taken up with what tries to superficially enhance our life. Nothing can compare with what God has created in His awesome and breathtaking ways: the pounding surf upon the jagged coastline boulders ... the awe-inspiring beauty of the ever changing colors of the Grand Canyon ... the rough and rugged magnificence of the rocky mountains ... the untold beauty of a sunset encased by brilliant multicolored clouds ... or the vast field of colorful flowers, each distinguished in shape, form, texture, and color. We stand speechless trying to comprehend **His voice in the wilderness**.

We are refreshed, inspired and blessed by His touch everywhere we look. David knew something of God's Majesty and wrote, *"Great is the Lord, and greatly to be praised; and His greatness is unsearchable (beyond our knowing, incomprehensible, unbelievable)"* (Ps. 145:3). David knew what it was to stand in the *tranquility of His Presence* and behold God in His awesome Majesty even amidst the clamor and hate that were incensed against Him. He experienced what it meant to, *"Be still and know that I am God"* (Ps. 46:10). O that we might experience what it means to be in *"the beauty of His holiness"* and hear **His voice in the wilderness.**

It is beyond our comprehension to behold His intricacy and immeasurable greatness in creation. From the infinitely small creatures to the magnificence of His greatest creations is unbelievable. Can we in any way understand the varied complexity of ants, butterflies, fish, boring beetles, and the vast array of animals, each with their distinct character, instincts, and habits? To behold the trillions of stars and the endless Universe is incomprehensible. This can be said of all of His creation in all the realms that He has created. It is **His voice in the Wilderness.**

However infinite is the magnitude of His creation, it does not compare to the greatest of all His creations. His Infinite transcending love that transforms the heart and life of sinful man to the praise of His glory *surpasses all of His creation.*

Man is steeped in sin, without God and without hope, determined to go his own way by rejecting His love, spurning His grace, and turning his back on God's long suffering and mercy. Mankind is not receptive to anything pertaining to God; therefore **man has chosen his own fate and eternal destiny.** *This is not God's choice ... it is man's choice from a rebellious, deceiving, self-centered heart.*

God, in His infinite grace, stands with open arms ready to receive and forgive the vilest of sinners. Ready to reconcile the sinner to Him to be part of the family of God. He wants to bring the sinner back to that for which he was created for ... *to love God and enjoy Him forever.* God has done everything necessary to make man a new creation by His grace. *"For He (God) hath made Him (Jesus Christ) to be sin for us, who knew no sin; that we might be made the righteousness of God in Him"* (2 Cor. 5:21). This is **His voice in the Wilderness.**

So Blessed!

Watchman Nee, the compelling Chinese evangelist, wrote these deeply spiritual words that are so significant: *"Nothing is so blessed as when our outward efforts cease and our attitudes become unforced ... when our words, prayers, and our very lives become* **spontaneous and sincere expressions of the life of Christ within.*"*

Proclaiming God's Word under adverse conditions, Watchman Nee *searched within* to see how intense his commitment of faith in Jesus Christ really was. He realized that his spiritual life was not to be obsessed with insincere expressions or a deceitful lifestyle, but a life and walk fully dedicated to the Lordship and Authority of Christ. His life must be the manifestation of **"Christ living within"** that fashioned his motives and attitude. This was the passion of his heart that brought such an intimate relationship where his words, prayers, and very life were *spontaneous and sincere expressions of the life of Christ within.*

There was no need to devise what he was to say or to make sure his life was in accordance to what he believed, it was apparent to sight and understanding to all. There was no pretense or superficial effort to be anything but what he was. His surrendered life was a transparent dedication to Jesus Christ as his Lord and Savior. The Holy Spirit moved through his daily walk without self-effort on his part. *It was the natural flow of an unwavering faith that walked in the conscious presence of Christ.* Humility of heart and a pure spirit embraced his life as God used him to move countless Chinese to fully trust the Lord.

When I meditated on this simple but profound statement and the effect it had on his life, I searched my heart and asked, "Is this true in my life? Are my words, prayers and life *spontaneous and sincere expressions of the life of Christ within* ... or do I respond in word and walk by preconceived motives and attitudes provoked by self?"

Spontaneous and sincere expressions disclose a firm, steadfast, personal relationship that knows no compromise or concessions of self-interests or gain. Our expressions and daily walk disclose who we are and reveal the depth of our spiritual life as we converse with others. Unconditional surrender to His Lordship of our will and life will reflect freedom, liberty, and truth. Godly virtues embrace the depth of our faith, the integrity of our heart, and sincerity of how we live. Such a dedication does not entertain hypocrisy, duplicity, or insincerity but is a transparent life of trust, faith, and obedience.

We are so blessed when we walk in His glorious companionship without any impediments to distract or divert our focus or life. When He is on the throne of our heart, in control of our life and empowering us in all of our being, *we will never be the same!* Our life will be an exciting journey, manifesting the fruit of the Spirit and being lived to the glory of His Name ... spontaneously and sincerely.

It is *Christ in us and we in Christ* that radically changes our life. That work of grace is not a matter of intellectual consent to spiritual truth but a *renovation of our heart and life by God*. Our thoughts, attitude, motives and precepts are completely changed as the nature of Christ becomes real and alive in our soul. It is then ... ***"Our outward efforts cease and our attitudes become unforced ... when our words, prayers and our very lives become spontaneous and sincere expressions of the Life of Christ within." So Blessed!***

This Is The Captain Speaking

The first time my wife and I took a cruise, I was somewhat fascinated when the intercom came on with a couple of sounds of the ship's horn and then a voice ... *"This is the Captain Speaking."* He welcomed us aboard and then gave us various information regarding the ship and our current cruising position, etc. Later, after several of these occurrences, we began to imitate the Captain, and it was rather an amusing situation.

We got a message from the Captain when we encountered some stormy weather. He assured us that we were in good hands and on a very safe ship. We felt secure with his reassuring words. It was comforting to know he had cruised this course and many others before. His experience and wisdom as an excellent seaman calmed our fears, and soon the waters became calm as we travelled on.

I thought how such an experience relates to the journey we are taking through life. Certainly, we all have encountered the stormy circumstances that often cause us to be fearful, terrified, and alarmed as we face the unknown, unexpected, and startling events of life. We often do not know where to turn, who to call, or what we should do. That is when the <u>*reality of our faith*</u> stands starkly before us.

Has our faith been shallow because we have never had an occasion to test it? We have said how wonderful God's promises are, how comforting and assuring, but we have not had to *make them real* in a devastating situation. We have cruised in calm seas and beautiful weather in our journey ... BUT NOW, we face difficulty we do not know how to handle! This is where the "rubber hits the road," when the reality of our faith is put to the test ... **"This is THE CAPTAIN Speaking."**

Do we really believe God's irrevocable promises as His voice resounds and reminds us of His Presence, Provisions, Care and Comfort ... as our Strong Tower, Defender and Mighty God? Often we respond with a doubtful <u>*yes*</u> but inside we know our faith is weak and lacking to trust Him fully. We can't <u>*let go of our carnal resources*</u> ... we can't face the tragedy of the present in our own strength ... we fail so miserably by not simply *"Cast(ing) all our anxieties on Him"* (1 Peter 5:7).

Are you ready to claim these verses? *"But now, this is what the Lord (THE CAPTAIN) says, who created you ... He who formed you: Fear not, for* **I have redeemed you; I have summoned you by name; you are mine.** *When you pass through the waters,* **I will be with you;** *and when you pass through the rivers,* **they will not sweep over you.** *When you walk through the fire,* **you will not be burned;** *the flames will not set you ablaze.* **For I am the Lord, your God, the Holy One of Israel, your Savior"** (Isa. 43:1-3). Has this been a promise we delight in and one that *anchors our faith*?

Our faith is real when it is tested in the trials of our life. It's one thing to talk about our faith but quite another to put true faith into practical application, and trust God in the devastating encounters we face. These testing times challenge our spiritual integrity and awaken us to the reality of where we are spiritually.

When we exercise true faith, we take God at His word, embrace truth, and apply it to our life. *Faith knows no bounds or staggers at the promises of God or the declarations of His grace. Faith reaches out to the unknown, the unseen, and the unimaginable and claims the impossible!* ... **"This is THE CAPTAIN Speaking."**

How Are You Investing Your Time?

How often we have said, "Where did the time go? It seems like only yesterday we took that trip"? This is especially true as we get older ... time just flies. Remember when you said, "Do you realize it's July already?" We wonder where our precious time went.

Time is something we cannot buy, sell, or bargain for. It has its way in all of our lives, and the question that faces all of us is: *"Are we squandering our time in meaningless behavior, or ... are we '**investing our time**' in meaningful and eternal issues?"* Someone wisely said, *"Time is God's gift to us ... how we spend it is our gift to God."*

Why is <u>time</u> so important? *Because it will never pass our way again.* The moments we had today are gone, never to return. Today is all we have. **"We have this moment to hold in our hand, it falls through our fingers like grains of sand. Yesterday is gone and tomorrow may never come ... but we have this moment Today."** (Bill Gaither).

How precious are the moments we have when our health is good, our energy is strong, and our vision is filled with the excitement of life! We are filled with exhilaration of fantasized expectation that seems to obliterate the *frailty of life*. We will not always be so fortunate: accidents, sickness, unexpected reverses, and depressing circumstances can bring clouds of despair, discouragement, and defeat. It is then we long for those precious moments when we were not encumbered with the sad realities of life. Often we have wished to recall those moments in time we spent so foolishly.

We are often taken up with life's responsibilities enforced upon us, and we fail to realize where we are in this time-frame of life's brevity. David said, *"We spend our years as a tale that is told"* (Ps. 90:9). As a boy, I remember anxiously waiting for the evening newspaper. I loved to read the comic section, which featured "Dick Tracy" with all of his unusual characters. The ending frame each day had these words written rather small ... *"To be continued."* Each day I would follow the story with excitement and curiosity.

Since then, I have given this little phrase much thought. *One day it will read ...* **The End.** *Life, as we know it today, will abruptly end, and we cannot look back, recall or relive those opportunities; God enables us to use our time in a meaningful and fruitful way ... being a blessing to others.* How hallowed when we have *invested our life* with eternal values in view ... encouraging someone whose heart has been broken ... standing beside one to let them know that God cares ... speaking a word that will bring a smile and joy in their life.

What is life all about? *It's about making every day an opportunity to embrace another with the "love of Christ"* ... lifting up those in despair ... being sensitive of their need ... sharing your life as a *"vessel of the Lord"* through which HE can flow freely with life-giving waters to refresh and restore another. *"Seize the moment"* God places before us.

While waiting to see the doctor, a middle-aged lady was wheeled into the room for an emergency X-ray. You could tell she was in great pain. Someone, also waiting to be seen, *"seized the moment"* and went over to pray for her. A stranger? Yes, ... but a life in great anxiety who needed God's touch on her life and the encouragement that someone cared for her. We cannot recall these *opportunities God puts in our path* ... we must *seize them*, for time waits for no one ... it will not pass our way again. *May we cherish our time ... use it wisely and with prudence ... and open our hearts to all God wants to do in the time He gives to us. Invest your life for eternity!* **Christ lives within us that He might live through us.**

The Ways Of God

Have you ever imagined what you would do if you were God? How would you create mankind with all the marvels of our brain, heart, lungs, our intricate blood system, muscles, and the many other magnificent and varied parts of our body? Would we have created memory, motives, attitudes, thought, speech, hearing, feeling and eyesight? *When we focus on the Majesty of God ... we are lost in the wonder of it all!* These are **the Ways of God!**

Our thoughts cannot imagine or envision the wonder of God. *"Through faith we understand that the worlds were framed by the word of God, so that things which are seen were not made by things that do appear"* (Heb. 11:3). Everything God made was *created from nothing.* Can you fathom that? No, it is inconceivable! These are **the Ways of God!**

Before the beginning of time, God already was. He is separate from all things, yet permeates all things. He had no origin; He is eternal, always was and will always be. We cannot fathom this fundamental truth, but *by faith we can believe it.* God, being able to <u>create</u>, was able to bring into existence elements that never were. It is not putting together rudiments to form something new. God spoke out of eternity ... existence out of non-existence ... and material out of the immaterial. He spoke, and immediately there were earth, plants, stars, water, flowers, animals and mankind. Man can invent, develop, and make things from other elements ... *but only God can create something out of nothing!* These are **the Ways of God!**

When you consider the miracles of God in the Bible, we stand in awe of His creative thought and actions. When Israel was pursued by Pharaoh's vast army and was enclosed by mountains on both sides and the Red Sea before them, God parted the sea, and they crossed it on *dry ground*. When Pharaoh's army pursued after them, God unleashed the waters, and the waters consumed the complete army. These are **the Ways of God!**

Consider the strange battle plan God gave Joshua to follow as he attacked Jericho. Following in obedience, the walls of Jericho fell, which led to victory. Also, the divine protection of the three young Hebrew men who refused to bow and worship the king and his golden idol. Thrown into the fiery furnace for noncompliance, they were not consumed, nor was the smell of smoke upon them. On so many other occasions, God's ways are beyond our imagination to protect, lead, and care for His own. Miraculous ... these are **the Ways of God!**

"For my thoughts are not your thoughts, neither are your ways my ways, saith the Lord" (Isa. 55:8). God has promised to be our sufficiency for our every need (2 Cor. 3:5) ... When we are weak and weary, He is our strength (Ps. 46:1-2) ... When oppressed by the enemy, He is our mighty fortress (Ps. 18:2) ... When the heathen rage, He is our Refuge (Ps. 27:5) ... When we are bewildered and know not the way or the decision to make, He is our faithful Guide (Prov. 3:5-6) ... When friend or foe attack us, He is our Hiding Place (Ps. 32:7). These are **the Ways of God!**

In the closing verses of Psalm 91 we read, *"I will rescue him ... I will protect him ... I will answer him ... I will be with him... I will deliver him ... I will honor him ... I will satisfy him ... I will show him my salvation."* Garrisoned ... Protected ... Blessed! All ours in Christ*!* **Only God can bring us to know Him from doubt to implicit trust ... from sorrow to glorious joy ... from despair to an intimacy in Christ ... from sure defeat to triumphant victory! These are the Ways of God!**

By This I Know

There are few things in life we can be certain of, regarding our journey through the alarming discords we face daily. We have no assurance of tomorrow, no guarantee of good health, that our finances will greatly diminish by unforeseen circumstances, or many other things we take for granted. Life is uncertain at best, fragile and subject to the complex nature of life itself.

When God sent Elijah to the widow's house in Zarephath, after many days, her son was sick and died. She was distraught and distressed. Elijah interceded with God for her son, and his life was restored. *"And the women said unto Elijah, Now **by this I know** that thou art a man of God"* (1 Kings 17:24).

When I read this account, I was prompted to take an introspective look at my life and ask, "When people see my life, hear my words, examine my walk ... do they say, '***by this I know*** you are a man of God'? ... Or do they see a compromised inconsistent life that is offensive and repulsive to them?" When my walk betrays what I profess ... my life speaks so loudly that people do not hear what I say.

When my spiritual life reflects the *virtues of Christ*, they will be convinced by my dedication and obedience that HE is my Lord and Authority, and His Life is reflected in my life. What a difference!

What did the widow of Zarephath see in Elijah? She knew he lived in close communion with God. When he prayed and interceded for her son, she knew he had touched the heart of God. There was no insincerity or superficiality in his walk but rather a transparent life that reflected the love of God and the reality of his faith in the God of his life!

How imperative is such a life today when so many Believers' lives are far from what God wants them to be. It seems that their relationship with the Lord is an *obligation* rather than the *incredible joy* of walking in blessed communion with Him each day. To them, the Lord is but a "symbol of truth" rather than the *Living Christ within our lives*. They live on the perimeter of Truth rather than being at the core where Truth is the integral and essence of their very life.

The world has seen enough of a shallow profession; they want to see a life *possessed by the Holy Spirit*, where He flows freely and fully through their lives. They have heard enough of the shame of meaningless prayer; they want to hear a Believer whose *prayers move the heart and power of God*. They are disgusted with the insincerity and hypocritical life of Believers who compromise their faith and seek the approval of man.

They want to be persuaded by a Believer who *stands with unwavering trust in God* and would give their life rather than renounce their faith! They want to be convinced by a life through which the *Spirit of God has full authority and a faith that is committed without hesitation to His Will* in every phase of their life!

Such a life is seen by the stalwart Believers in Hebrews 11 and the martyrs of the faith throughout the past ages who gave their life to be burned at the stake, suffered incredibly at the hands of sinful men, and endured as seeing Him who is the eternal and faithful Lord of their life.

O that we might manifest the virtues of Christ through our life that it becomes *a spontaneous and sincere expression of His Life lived through us*. Others can say of us as the widow at Zarephath said of Elijah... ***"by this I know you are a man of God."***

In All These Things

The Believer faces various circumstances daily that challenge his faith, his commitment and dedication to the Lord. Sometimes we think they are separating us from the love of God. But Paul says, *"Nay,* **in all these things** *we are more than conquerors through Him that loved us."*

What things is Paul referring to? He answers, *"For I am persuaded, that neither death, nor life, nor angels, nor principalities nor powers, nor things present, nor things to come, nor height, nor depth, nor any other creature, shall be able to separate us from the love of God, which is in Christ Jesus our lord"* (Rom. 8:37-39).

These things can and do separate us from our *fellowship* with the Lord, from an *intimate walk* with Christ and from a *oneness of Spirit* with Him and other Believers. But *these things* cannot separate us from the *love of God.* The bedrock of our faith rests in the marvel of God's infinite love manifested on the Cross of Calvary.

There is a difference between our **security** *in Christ* and our **walk** *with Christ.* Our **security** *in Christ* rests on the validity of His Word and the might of His power. Our **walk** *with Christ* depends on our **obedience** to His commands and the **sincerity** of our commitment to Him. When we walk with Christ, He enables us to be *"more than conquerors through Him that loved us."*

What are *these things* that interrupt, discourage and defeat our walk and intimacy with Christ and others? When our self-centered life governs our motives and attitudes, it affects our relationship and disrupts a *Unity of Spirit* with Christ. We live within the boundaries of our self-imposed bondage. Pride, ego, self-independence, arrogance, vanity, self-centeredness, and a host of other ungodly characteristics manifest an offensive and obnoxious spirit. *These things* should not be a part of a Believer's life.

Look at the things that are the *building blocks of a Unity of Spirit,* which honors the Lord and establishes a blessed intimacy and fellowship with Him. True Believers are distinguished by *spiritual integrity.* They seek to have a life focused on the Lord: to know and actively apply the principles and precepts of God's Word to every phase of their life. They come before the Lord with a pure heart and a contrite spirit that they may be filled to overflowing with the love of God. The vessel must be clean, our motives made pure, and our attitude righteous if Christ is to be magnified in our life.

Can there be a greater joy than to walk with the Lord ... dare to trust Him fully ... commune with Him in the secret place of His presence ... see Him *"do exceeding abundantly more that we can ask or even think through His power that is at work within you"* (Eph. 3:20) ... supply all our need according to His riches in glory through by Christ Jesus ... and live in the realization that our life is in His hands? Wow! What an incredible life we have in Christ!

God uses the difficulties, adversities, and trials of life not only to *define the reality of our faith,* but also to *build us up and mature us in the faith.* He will take our bitter experiences and turn them into songs of deliverance, our weakness into His strength, and our finite foresight into visions of glory. It is **"in all these things ... we are more than conquerors ... through Him that loved us"** (Rom. 8:37).

Burn Your Bridges

Paul knew something about *"burning your bridges."* We have difficulty with this. Paul said, *"Forgetting those things which are behind and reaching forth unto those things which are before"* (Phil. 3:13). The *passion of his life* after he was radically transformed by the power of God was, **"That I may know Him"** (Phil. 3:10). Paul studied under Gamaliel to understand, in a measure, the infinite love of God in sending His Son, Jesus Christ, to pay the debt of our sin. He wanted to know the <u>*thought of God*</u>, whose greatness and Majesty are inconceivable, whose love, mercy, and grace are infinite.

One basic principle he learned was that *we cannot do what only God can do and that God will not do what we can do.* "That I may know Him" requires effort, commitment, discipline, and taking the initiative to work out the salvation that God has worked in us. James said, *"faith by itself, if it is not accompanied by action, is dead"* (James 2:17). *We* must establish our character and meaningful habits.

The ungodly past in Paul's life was a dreadful confrontation to him after he met God on the way to Damascus to imprison more Christians. How blessed it was when God revealed to him that *"where sin abounded, grace did much more abound"* (John 5:21). Paul's sin was nailed to the Cross and forgiven by Christ. He was unshackled from his past offenses and now was *"reaching forth unto those things which are before. I press toward the mark for the prize of the high calling of God in Christ Jesus"* (Phil. 3:13-14).

Often we are burdened down by our devastating past and think <u>*we*</u> need to *make restitution to God for our destructive words, action, or attitude.* This puts a tremendous burden on our spiritual journey. We do not embrace the fact that ***Jesus Christ atoned for all our sin, past, present and future, on Calvary.*** We cannot attain what only God can do. John said, *"If we (freely) admit that we have sinned and confess our sin, He is faithful and just (true to His own nature and promises) and will forgive our sins (dismiss our lawlessness) and* **continuously cleanse us from all unrighteousness** *... everything not in conformity to His will and purpose, thought and action"* (1 John 1:9) (Amp.Ver.).

We are unshackled *to* freedom, peace, and hope. We need to *"burn our bridges"* of the past, not let them *"hang on"* as if *we* had to atone for them. **God has done that.** Do not let Satan use these past malicious measures to defeat our spiritual journey today. Take the initiative. Take God at His word. Like Paul: *"Forgetting those things which are behind and reaching forth unto those things which are before."*

Well do I know my own sinfulness, but I also know the virtue of His cleansing blood. I know my weakness, but I also know the all-sufficiency of His grace to be my strength and power. I know the limitations of my finite resources, but I also know the boundless resources of His grace. I know the treachery of my own deceitful heart, but I also know *"that He who hath begun a good work in you will carry it on to completion until the day of Christ Jesus"* (Phil. 1:6).

I know it is not I, but His life that lives in me that enables me to be triumphant and victorious in every phase of my life. Burn your bridges (commit the past to His cleansing blood) and live triumphantly in Christ! This is God's Way!

Rise To The Occasion

Every day offers occasions that will challenge our spiritual life and will verify or contradict our commitment to the Lord. We are often amiss knowing how the world keenly observes the actions and reactions Believers exercise in their everyday walk. I think unbelievers are more aware of the *"demands of discipleship"* than we are. They are quick to point out where we have fallen, given into carnal, fleshly concerns, or compromised in what we profess to believe.

We rest in the security of our salvation rather than adhere to Paul's admonition, *"work out our own salvation with fear and trembling"* (Phil. 2:12). **What are we saved for?** *That Jesus Christ may be manifested in our mortal flesh to the praise of His glory.* How can we do that? Certainly not by a humdrum, "status quo" spiritual life. We see too many Believers today that are examples of this sort of life.

Every Believer should *"rise to the occasion"* to be all God wants them to be! This demands the surrender of our heart and will to the Authority and Lordship of Christ. Paul reveals to the Believers at Corinth, *"Do you not know that your body is the temple (the very sanctuary) of the Holy Spirit Who lives within you, Whom you have received (as a gift) from God?* **You are not your own.** *You were bought for a price (purchased with a preciousness and paid for, made His own).* **So then, 'honor God and bring glory to Him in your body'"** (1 Cor. 6:19-20).

Without any elaboration, we should know what that means. Yet, the majority of Believers do not relate to the fact that Jesus Christ *purchased the ownership of our life* from the condemnation and consequences of our sin, from the chains of slavery ... to being reconciled to God. He has done what we could not do. We are His ... by Creation, by Redemption, and by His Grace. Be receptive to the Holy Spirit as He seeks to **manifest the life of Christ in every phase of our life.**

How can we do that? We yield our will to His absolute Sovereign Rule and Authority of our life ... unrestricted and unconditionally ... not legalistically, but in *surrendered loving response.* Paul wrote, *"I have been crucified with Christ (in Him); I have shared His crucifixion;* ***it is no longer I who live, but Christ, the Messiah, lives in me;*** *and the life I now live in the body I live by faith (by adherence to and reliance on and complete trust) in the Son of God, Who loved me and gave Himself up for me"* (Gal. 2:20) (Amp.Ver.). God replaces our sinful and selfish rule as He reigns on the throne of our heart.

"For the love of Christ controls and urges and impels us ... so that all those who live (by faith in Him) might live no longer to and for themselves, but to and for Him who died and was raised again for their sakes ... therefore if any person is (engrafted) in Christ, the Messiah, he is (a new creature altogether) a new creation; the old (previous moral and spiritual condition) has passed away. Behold, the fresh and new has come" (1 Cor. 5:14-15, 17) (Amp.Ver.). **God has created us anew by His power** ... refocused our vision ... given us a new beginning, a new life, and a blessed hope as we walk in holy companionship with the Lord. Fix our eyes upon the Author and Finisher of our faith!

Rise to the Occasion and seize the blessed opportunity *to let Him rule and reign supreme in our life!* We are here to submit to His will that we may be *"conformed to the image of His Son"* (Rom. 8:29). God will make us broken bread and poured out wine to feed and nourish others and glorify His Name through us.

"Walk Before Me"

(Gen. 17:1)

Never make the mistake of trying to forecast the way God is going to answer our prayer. *God's ways are past finding out. He leads according to His plan and purpose.* Looking back into our lives, we can see time and again how His way was so different than what we would have chosen. His way was divine wisdom, foresight and for our good and His glory.

God never spoke to Abraham for thirteen years as he dwelt in Haran. He had gone there to seek nourishment rather than *trusting God in the famine* that swept through his land. Not until every self-centered motivation, self-independence, intelligent understanding, and finite reasoning *was at an end*, did God speak and renew His covenant with Abraham and said, **"I am God Almighty (El Shaddai), walk before me, and be thou perfect"** (Gen. 17:1).

Was there ever a more heart-wrenching test as when, in obedience to God, Abraham lifted up his hand to slay his son as a sacrifice unto Him? Isaac was the *"son of promise, his only son, the son whom he loved."* As he raised his hand to slay Isaac, the angel of God said to Abraham, *"Lay not thine hand upon the lad, neither do thou anything unto him: for **now I know** that thou fearest God, seeing thou hast not withheld thy son, thine only son, from me"* (Gen. 22:12). **"I am God Almighty, walk before me and be thou perfect"**.

How did God prepare Moses to lead Israel through the wilderness for 40 years? He took him to the backside of the desert in Midian.

God spoke to him from a burning bush that was not consumed. How strange are the ways and will of God. It was in the solitude of the Midian desert Moses was broken before God of His self-reliance and pretentious attitude until he was ready to **"walk before God"** with unwavering faith.

Faith never knows where or how it is being led: it knows and loves the One Who is leading. *Walking with God* does not question, doubt or debate God's Hand upon our life. When we surrender our will to Him without reservation, we will not desire to trust in ourselves ... but **trust Him alone!** It is always a marvelous wonder to see His Hand making the crooked ways straight, moving the mountains, and parting the sea of our devastating encounters. Such will be our experience when we **"walk before God"** in His glorious companionship each day.

It is Christ in us and we in Christ that radically changes our life: it is a renovation of our heart and life by God. Our thoughts, attitude, motives and precepts are completely changed as the *nature of Christ becomes alive in our soul.*

"Jesus now has many lovers of His heavenly kingdom, but few bearers of His cross. He has many who desire consolation, but few who desire tribulation. He finds many companions of His table, but few of His abstinence. All desire to rejoice in Him, but few are willing to endure anything for Him or with Him. Many follow Jesus to the breaking of bread, but few to the drinking of the cup of His passion. Many revere His miracles, but few follow the humiliation of the cross" (Thomas A. Kempis).

Our **walk before Him** should be a mystery to the world. A Christ-centered life, the source of our strength, the grounds of our confidence, the reason for our actions, and the steadfastness of our faith should bewilder them. May our walk before God be the passion of our life! **"I am Almighty God, walk before me, and be thou perfect."**

Every Thought Into Captivity

Why do we find so few Believers manifest in their spiritual journey a life that is <u>*spiritually natural*</u>? There seems to be an inconsistency in what they profess and the life they live. Often there is a pretense, insincerity or superficial façade that comes through rather than simply a life that reveals a depth of God's love and is *spiritually natural*. Why is this? *It all has to do with our personal relationship with Jesus Christ and understanding of His work of grace in our lives.*

What does it mean to be <u>spiritually natural</u>? It means that God is in control of our life, and our spiritual response comes *naturally*. There is no question as to what we should do, act or say. We have read God's Word and know the desire of His heart. The Holy Spirit gives us divine discernment to apply God's desire to every phase of our life.

We are <u>*spiritually natural*</u> when we respond in ways that glorify His Name. We exchange our self-serving life to live for Him without restraint or compromise. It is having our life *"focused on Christ"* and **His Life lived through us.**

This can only come from the radical renovation of our heart by God. *But it goes deeper than just being a Believer.* There must be the complete surrender of our will to His Lordship and Authority. This means **we exchange <u>our</u> will for <u>His</u> will to control our life.** *"You are not your own, we have been bought with a price, therefore glorify God in your body, and in your spirit, which are God's"* (1 Cor. 6:19-20). God changes our attitude, priorities, and response to the Holy Spirit, as *we are captivated by the compelling love of God.* Our spiritual journey seeks to be adorned with the disposition and virtues of Christ. We face satanic warfare in His might and power demolishing the strongholds of Satan.

Paul wrote an admonition to the Believers in Corinth: *"For though we walk (live) in the flesh, we are not carrying on our warfare according to the flesh and using mere human weapons. For the **weapons of our warfare** are not physical (weapons of flesh and blood), but they are **mighty before God** for the overthrow and destruction of strongholds, (inasmuch as we) refute arguments and theories and reasonings and every proud and lofty thing that sets itself up against the (true) knowledge of God; and **we lead every thought and purpose away captive into the obedience of Christ***" (2 Cor. 10:3-5)(Amp.Ver.).

Why is it necessary to surrender our life to God's Authority and control? Because we are in warfare with one who is greater than we, whose primary objective is to discourage, defeat, and destroy us from any personal relationship with Jesus Christ. His deceiving and cunning ways will infiltrate into our lives if we are not *"protected by the full armor of God"* (Eph. 6:13-18). He initiates doubt, frustration, confusion, and disbelief regarding Jesus Christ and His Word to us. What is the answer to our dilemma?

Take God at His word; apply His irrevocable promises to our spiritual life; stand with unwavering faith in the Faithful One. Renounce every attack of Satan in the Name of Jesus. **"Lead every thought and purpose away captive into the obedience of Christ."** We can only do this in God's strength, discernment and mighty power. *To let go of our life with all of its finite limitation ... is to gain His Life in all its fullness, sufficiency and glory.*

*Where there is **unerring wisdom** to direct our way, **almighty power** to execute His plan, a **receptive and responsive spirit** to follow His leading, ... **no difficulty can exist which cannot be overruled by His Power.***

Good Or Best?

I wonder how many times we have settled for a _good_ thing, place, or experience ... when, with patience, discernment, and God's leading, we could have had the God's _best?_ We can all recall experiences where we have been too anxious when *patience and faith* would have served us better. Our decisions are occasionally prompted by impulse, emotions or by our overzealous desires. We are so prone to enter into a decision or experience ... *"where angels fear to tread"* (Alexander Pope).

One of the defining features that we often lack, as we face meaningful occasions, is *Patience.* Have you ever stood on the beach where large boulders graced the shoreline and were awestruck by the furious pounding waves crashing against the huge rocks? They stood firm and withstood the onslaughts of the waves, day after day. We should respond with such steadfast firmness and with *perseverance, faith, and patience ...* as we wait upon God to lead us in His will.

Patience is not indifference, but a *vision* of what God can and will do if we *"wait on the Lord."* Isaiah wrote, **"But they that wait on the Lord** *shall renew their strength; they shall mount up with wings as eagles; they shall run and not be weary; and they shall walk and not faint"* (Isa. 40:31). **God is the source of patience** and imparts moral inspiration when our reach exceeds our grasp. This is one of the secrets of having *not just the good, but* **God's Best.**

Moses *"endured as seeing Him Who is invisible."* Spiritually, a man with a _vision_ is not committed to some ideal or cause, but is dedicated without reservation **to God Himself.** When we have the inspiration of the vision of God, we will see Him do things only He can do. *God will give us His Best* ... more than we can experience within ourselves. We can have *God's Best* when our spiritual life finds reality by a life **surrendered to God** ... a life **controlled by God** ... and *a life lived for God! Let's briefly examine each one:*

A life surrendered to God: This is the last citadel we refuse to let go. This determines who is going to control our life. We cherish the thought that <u>we</u> call the shots, determine what <u>we</u> want, and <u>we</u> are not willing to relinquish control of our prized possession. This is motivated by selfish independence and selfish desires. If we are to have **God's Best**, it is imperative that we *surrender our right to manage our life to God Himself.*

A life controlled by God: He knows our strength and weaknesses, what lies ahead, and how devastating occurrences will impact our life. What better life can we have when we let the Omnipotent One, God Himself, direct our lives? Solomon wrote, *"Lean on, trust and be confident in the Lord with all your heart and mind, and do not rely on your own insight or understanding. In all of your ways, know, recognize, and acknowledge Him, and He will direct and make straight and plain your paths"* (Prov. 3:5-6) (Amp.Ver.).

A life lived for God: Seeking to live for God means the persevering pursuit to abide in Him, to walk faithfully in the Spirit, to engage in true meaningful prayer and fervent meditation of His Word. There must be within our heart the hunger and thirst to follow Him fully and to the Holy Spirit drawing us into an intimate personal relationship with Christ. There are no short cuts, neither is it a one-time attainment, but a <u>*becoming life*</u> of controlled discipline.

A life lived for God is a daily surrender of our will to His Lordship and resting in the sufficiency and work of God's grace to mold our lives to the "image of His Son." It is then we will have not just what is good ... but GOD'S BEST!

When Day Is Done

We often recall the events of the day, which now pass into Eternity. The moments we had today have been spent either in significant building *or* relinquishing meaningful time as a "*status quo*" existence ... to be a blessing to others *or* living a mundane ordinary life ... to be consumed with our selfish desires *or* fix our eyes, heart, and spirit on Jesus. We have been motivated by our selfish nature *or* yielded our life to His authority to be "*made in the image of His Son*" (Rom. 8:29). **When day is done ... what have been our choices?**

We have *this day* ... it will not pass our way again. How blessed it is to yield each day to His Leading, opening up our hearts to opportunities that will come our way, and be an instrument used for His Glory ... see Him do things through us that only He can do ... and experience God molding our lives to glorify Him in all of our life. It is an exciting adventure of faith to trust The One Who created the universe and holds it all together. Do we reflect on His Love, His Grace, and the inconceivable blessing of having walked with the Lord today! **When Day is Done ... what have been our thoughts?**

Time passes in an unprecedented swiftness, especially as we grow older. Our life is unpredictable, uncertain, a brief time without any assurance of another day. It is important to live to the maximum and buy up every opportunity for His Glory. May eternal values motivate our choices, enhance our walk, and stimulate our desires to live each day with our focus on doing His Will, plan, purpose and be pliable to His leading. "*Whereas you know not what shall be on the morrow. For what is your life? It is even as a vapor, that appears for a little time, and then vanishes away"* (James 4:14). **When Day is Done ... how did we use our invaluable time?**

What is the viewpoint God has given us? What is our purpose for being here? It is that we may be captives in the way of Christ's triumphs ... that we may glorify Him as the Holy Spirit works through us. Paul said, I am in the way of a *"conqueror through Him that loved us"* (Rom. 8:37). It mattered not what the circumstances were, how often he was buffeted and beaten by his adversaries, he was always led in the way of triumph. *"Now thanks be unto God, which always causes us to triumph in Christ ..."* (2 Cor.2:14). **When day is done... did we walk with Christ triumphantly?**

Meditation is a most intense spiritual act as it brings our mind, heart and spirit submissive to Christ, where we are brought to a oneness in Him. The Holy Spirit makes our times of meditation precious and meaningful reflecting on our relationship with Christ and how He fits us into the mold of His plan. It's a time of being quiet before the Lord and having Him speak to our hearts ... of our reveling in His Majesty and infinite Greatness. He infuses into our heart the depth of His love, mercy, and grace that we might go forth renewed in spirit and strengthened by His Mighty Hand. **When day is done... was our meditation meaningful?**

There must be a laying aside of hindering weights before we can run the race that is set before us (Heb. 12:1). There must be a turning from the world before there can be a turning to the Lord (Isa. 55:7). There must be a putting off of the <u>old man</u> before there can be the putting on of the <u>new man</u> (Eph. 4:22-24). There must be a "denying ungodliness and worldly lusts" before we can "live soberly, righteously and godly in this present world" (Titus 3:12) ... (Arthur Pink). *"Be still and know that I am God"* (Ps. 46:10). Have we embraced the magnitude of His Love and Grace? *Live in the wonder of it all!* ... **When day is done... how have we responded to God?**

We Shall Behold Him

We have all experienced looking through sunglasses to protect our eyes from the penetrating rays of the sun. We see everything scaled down from its brightness and see things darkly. The Word of God says, *"For now we see through a glass, darkly; but then face to face: now I know in part; but then shall I know even as also I am known"* (1 Cor. 13:12). We cannot imagine what it will be like when He comes in all His glory; we shall see Him face to face. **We shall behold Him!**

All the terms in which God described His perfections, they may be focused on three major virtues: His Majesty, His Mercy, and His Justice. Let's look briefly at each one:

His Majesty: "God, in being the Lord God of all, proclaimed that He was the eternal, self-existing Being, which created all things and holds them together. He holds unlimited authority over all the works of His hands. His dominion is universal, His power irresistible, His Sovereignty unrestrained: He doeth according to His will throughout the universe and among the inhabitants of the earth. Until we have learned to appreciate His Sovereignty, shall we be able rightly to appreciate His love and mercy" (Charles Simeon). When we focus our hearts on the Majesty of God ... everything else loses its finite significance.

God waits patiently for us to enter into the *"secret of His presence"* that He may reveal unto us the magnitude of His Majesty and the exceeding enormity of His Glory. Let the Holy Spirit electrify our hearts with the incomprehensible Glory and Majesty of God. We will be lost in the wonder of it all and live in the might of His power. ***We shall behold Him!***

His Mercy: We understand that God's Mercy is withholding the judgment of our sin, which we rightly deserve. In contrast to His Mercy is His Amazing Grace, by which He gives unto us that which we do not deserve. Our Almighty God is abundant in goodness and truth and longsuffering. We see His Mercy and Grace throughout His Word as He dealt with Israel and the many "*chosen ones*" who fell to their selfish interests and lustful desires.

Look at the children of Israel who murmured and rebelled as He led them for forty years in the wilderness ... the lustful fall of David ... the rebellion of Jonah to follow God's command in obedience ... the arrogance of Peter at the Last Supper, who shortly thereafter denied the Lord three times. There are many more whom *God withheld His judgment and dealt with them in divine grace.* But the hallmark of His Grace is seen in "*forgiving our iniquity, transgression, and sin through Jesus Christ.*" How unfathomable is His Mercy and Grace! On His second coming ... ***We shall behold Him!***

His Justice: God takes delight in His Mercy, but He will never violate the rights of Justice: He will pardon but not the impenitent or unbelieving: it is only to those who will repent and believe the Gospel that He will finally approve Himself a reconciled God. God has done everything necessary to forgive and reconcile the sinner unto Himself. Many refuse His Love, reject His grace, and turn their back on His Mercy. If they will live and die in sin, they must "*eat the fruit of their own doing.*" ***God is,*** the Just, Holy, and Righteous One ... full of Mercy, Grace and Love ... ***We shall behold Him!***

The trumpet shall sound, the dead in Christ shall arise, and we, who are alive, shall ascend and meet Him, our Lord and Savior, and *forever be with Him*... ***King of kings and Lord of lords!*** ***We shall behold Him!***

Doing Good Or Walking With God?

When we ask others what's the difference between *"doing good"* and *"walking with God,"* we have a variety of answers. However, there is a distinct difference between the two. Good human characteristics are often seen in others as they seek to be a moral, principled, and ethical person. They seek to be a contributor to the community and this is commendable and should certainly embrace all of our lives. They are to be admired for their disciplined life and desire to reach out to others in need. However, *we must not confuse <u>good moral characteristics</u> with "<u>walking with God</u>."*

We can have a good moral character and not walk with God. In fact, many whose character displays these admirable traits do not have any interests in God at all. <u>*Good moral character*</u> is the result of man's determination and resolve to be morally correct and ethical in all his dealings while having a heart of compassion for those in need.

"Walking with God" begins with being reborn by God. This takes place when the Holy Spirit awakens us of our sin that has separated us from God. God has provided a way whereby we might be forgiven and reconciled to Him. Through repentance of our sin and receiving Christ as God's way of salvation, God exchanges our sinful nature with all of its "baggage" and gives us *His spiritual nature*. God empowers us to walk in His companionship. It is not <u>*our doing*</u> but *God's*. *We will manifest Divine characteristics in our life...* not just good human characteristics. *He will live His life through us...* not our human life trying to be godly. Doing good is initiated by our *human effort*. *"*Walking with God*" is initiated and empowered by*

God. The supernatural is made natural by His grace that works out in the practical details of our life.

*"According to His divine power (God) hath given to us all things that pertain unto life and godliness, through the knowledge of Him that hath called us to glory and virtue: Whereby are given unto us exceeding great and precious promises: that by these we might be **partakers of the divine nature**, having escaped the corruption that is in the world through lusts"* (2 Peter 1:3-4).

These verses reveal the vast difference of those who *"do good"* and those who *"walk with God."* It centers in our "point of reference." Those who limit their walk to *doing good* are bound within the walls of their own intelligence and natural resources. The effect of their life has its boundaries. Their understanding does not plumb the depths of spiritual understanding. God said, *"But the natural man receives not the things of the Spirit: for they are foolishness to them, because they are **spiritually discerned**"* (1 Cor. 2:14).

Those who *"walk with God"* have as their *"point of reference"* the Divine Character of God and the Validity of His Word. The *understanding in spiritual matters* is not from his human intellect, but from a heart and will walking in obedience to God. His walk <u>begins</u> with God and is enabled by God. He seeks His leading and the work of His mighty power in the inner man. He draws from the Divine resources of God's grace and applies them to all of his life daily.

There is a simplicity and calmness about God in working out His plans ... a divine resourcefulness in His power to overcome every difficulty we face ... an infinite compassion, care and concern in God that reaches to our every need ... a covenant with His own to which He is irrevocably committed ... and resources of His grace for every Believer that they may be *vessels of honor.* **This characterizes a man who "Walks With God."**

Rivers Of Living Water

What a beautiful picture God reveals of Jesus being the *Fountainhead and the Source* of refreshing life-giving water. In the measure we abide in Him, he promises that *"out of our innermost being shall flow rivers of living water"* (John 7:38). The water He gives to the Believer *is not for him,* but is to flow *from God through us* to encourage, inspire, and be a blessing to others.

Norman Grubb, the son-in-law of the great missionary to Africa, C. T. Studd, said, *"Being filled is not enough. We need to have a continuous* **overflow** *of the waters from the Fountainhead ... the virtues of Christ flowing through us to thirsty souls in immeasurable ways."* We are not to be like the Dead Sea, always taking in but never giving out. Someone wisely said, "Impression without expression leads to depression." The life-giving waters are not for *our* blessing or experience ... we are simply the *channel* that God uses to carry His irrepressible life and love to others.

Well might we ask the question, "How freely are these refreshing waters flowing through us?" When the water is not freely pouring out, there is a defect, a hindrance, or an impediment in our relationship with the Lord that is radically affecting the flow. The life-giving waters are His work of grace; *this is His doing, not ours.* Our spiritual disposition ... a clean heart and a pure receptive spirit ... determine the flow of God's refreshing waters. There should be nothing between our soul and our Savior.

I remember all to well when my irrigation (irritation) system was only giving out a third of the water it should. After investigation, I found a little pebble that was inhibiting the flow and was the cause of my grass turning brown. I thought how true this is in our spiritual life. The *"pebble of sin"* (Heb. 12:1), neglect, anger, an unforgiving spirit, unfaithfulness or some other hindrance can stifle the refreshing water from our *Fountainhead, Jesus Christ,* and we cease to be used of Him.

"Out of our innermost being shall flow rivers of living water." You might say, "I don't see the rivers." We are not to focus on results or solutions, but fix our eyes and hearts on HIM ... walk in obedience to His will and purpose. *"Obedience is our responsibility ... the results are His responsibility"* (Oswald Chambers).

God works through the obscure, the unknown, the ignored, ... but steadfastly the waters flow *through the channel that is receptive and responsive to His work of grace.* The Holy Spirit seizes that life and takes the broken pieces and makes something beautiful out of them. The rivers of His grace begin to flow freely to encourage, inspire and bless those that are hurting and in great need. How blessed it is when our flood gates are wide open and *"from our innermost being flow rivers of living water."*

We never know what lies within the heavy heart of those God brings across our path. There could be burdens that we would not dare to bear ... brokenness we would shun to experience ... and hopelessness we would not want to embrace. *God places these devastating needs in our path,* that we may be the channel through which *"rivers of living water"* meet a need and will be used in a life-changing way!

The Gospel is a mystery; the riches of His grace are inconceivable, the glory of God is incomprehensible and the blessed hope of the Believer is incredible. **May the "rivers of living waters" flow freely through us to lift up the fallen, encourage the down-trodden, and stand beside the weak. May we be that channel of blessing!**

Fret Not

Every Believer is faced with the challenge to open up their life and let God live His life through them. Paul wrote to the Believers in Corinth, *"What? know you not that your body is the temple of the Holy Ghost which is in you, which you have of God, and you are not your own? For you are bought with a price: therefore glorify God in your body, and in your spirit, which are God's"* (1 Cor. 6:19-20).

Few Believers fathom the meaning of these verses. Many profess to believe the cardinal truths of God's Word, but few plumb the depths of what it means to *"glorify God in your body, and in your spirit, which are God's."* Our daily walk so often contradicts what we profess. Our motives, attitude, and responses declare before all our relationship with the Lord.

<u>*Fretting*</u> *springs from a determination to get our own way.* It expresses turmoil, anguish, discord, and frustration within our hearts. It is one thing to say, *"Fret Not,"* but a very different thing for our disposition to yield this need to God and let Him live through us in such occasions. David said, *"Rest in the Lord, and wait patiently for him ... fret not thyself because of him who prospers in his way ... fret not thy self in any wise to do evil ... but those that wait on the Lord, they shall inherit the earth"* (Ps. 34:7-9).

Fretting, fussing, and excessive unwanted concern should not be part of our life as a Believer. All of our fretting and anxiety is an indication that we are not living under His Lordship and Authority and our daily walk is displeasing to Him. We face difficulties by leaving God out of our calculations. Such action of our carnal life always ends in sin. These are the times when we need to find our sufficiency in HIM. David faced many agonizing situations within his own personal life and from those that opposed him. But, David learned, as did Paul, to *"rest in the Lord"* (Ps. 37:7). Both confronted the anger and hostility of evil men and dealt with this sinful issue of <u>*fretting*</u> before they experienced God's ever-conquering Spirit. His abiding Spirit within made them a clean and clear channel through which God could use them to be an encouragement and blessing to others.

Paul writes, *"But thanks be to God, Who in Christ **always leads us in triumph** ... as trophies of Christ's victory ... and through us spreads and makes evident the fragrance of the knowledge of God everywhere"* (2 Cor. 2:14)(Amp.Ver.).

"Resting in the Lord" does not depend on external circumstances at all, but on our personal relationship to God Himself. This is a *"learning process"* in which, when faced with stressful encounters, we **"Cast all your care** (anxieties, trials, frustrations, anger) **on Him**, for He careth for you" (1 Peter 5:7). We must *learn* to let Him take control of our emotional response when we experience these situations.

When we *cast all our care on Him,* our *desires* will be fortified by His love and compassion; our *fears* will be relieved in view of His providence; *our anxiety will be overcome by His tender mercies and comfort.* In prayer, He quiets our troubled hearts, and an inexpressible calmness pervades our whole being. He will give to us a quietness of spirit and the confidence of His presence that will free us from the distress that all but consumes us. *When God overflows our cup, fear, anxiety, fretting and apprehension are overcome by His grace, as we rest, abide, and trust in His Sufficiency.*

Oh that the whole of our personality may be filled to overflowing by the Holy Spirit with the adequacy of Christ as we encounter God in true prayer.

Common Days And Common Ways

It is interesting to become aware of how most Believers think in regard to their walk with God. How different it is in God's evaluation. Most Believers, when they are saved, immediately want to <u>do something</u> for God. They want to be active contributors to the ministry, take part in some way to manifest what <u>they</u> can do for God. When Jesus called us to be His disciple, He said, *"If any man shall come after me, let him deny himself, and take up his cross daily, and follow me"* (Luke 9:24).

The Christian life is a difficult one. It is *identifying* our life with Christ. It is a life of *self-denial* and taking up <u>our</u> *cross* daily ... where He is our Lord and Authority. It is *not* living occasionally on a spiritual mountaintop experience, or projecting a life *we think* is spiritual, or trying to *impress* others with our dedication or spiritual façade.

The life of a *true Believer* that most glorifies the Lord is the life where **Christ lives His Life through us** on common days and common ways ... in an everyday normal way. We see this exemplified in the life of John the Baptist. We read that John the Baptist *"looked upon Jesus **as he walked** ..."* (John 1:36). Now what does that imply?

He was deeply impacted by the *way Jesus walked* each day in an ordinary common way. John the Baptist did not see Jesus perform miracles or spend all night in prayer. He did not watch Him on the Mount of Transfiguration or in any great moment but saw Him on an ordinary day and observed the *genuineness of His divine love and grace* that flowed from His life. *"And looking upon Jesus **as He walked**, he said, Behold the lamb of God"* (John 1:36).

As I wrote this, it prompted me to ask, *"What influence does my life portray as I walk before the world?* Do others see a carnal hypocritical life of a *professing* Believer? Do they see one that flaunts a spiritual life trying to impress others?" The world is disgusted with such superficial Believers. **God forbid** that our life should be so shallow, uncommitted, and not portray a clean heart and a pure, sincere spirit.

The world is impacted by Believers whose lives have been transformed by the grace of God, who display on common days and common ways their *identity with Christ*... taking up their cross daily and following the One who redeemed and reconciled them to God! These Believers are living in the reality of what Matthew wrote, *"For whosoever will save his life shall lose it: **but whosoever will lose his life for my sake the same shall find it**"* (Matt. 9:24).

The true Believer's priority is *"to know Christ,"* to identify with Him despite whatever abuse, persecution or suffering they must endure, and to open their life fully for **Christ to live through them**. Their life is *transparent*... in plain view for all to see, that in common days and common ways his life does not vary but is consistently and steadfastly surrendered to His Lordship and Authority.

True believers are distinguished by spiritual integrity. *He seeks to have his life focused on the Lord, to know and actively apply the truth, principles and precepts of God's Word to every phase of his life. He comes before God with a pure heart and a contrite spirit that he may be filled to overflowing with the love of God. Circumstances be what they may, their life always portrays the depth of their faith.*

Being embraced by the holiness of God should be the hallmark of our life and the distinguishing character of every Believer.

Work Out Your Own Salvation

In my early spiritual journey, I wondered what Paul meant when he wrote, *"Work out your own salvation with fear and trembling"* (Ph. 2:12). He was writing to those who had repented of their sin and received Jesus Christ as their Savior. We have been made a <u>new creation in Christ</u> by his supernatural transforming grace. The *"Living Christ"* has invaded our life and now lives within us. *We must work out what God has worked in.*

Paul is referring to the *development of our Christian character*. This involves maturing in our faith, developing an effectual sincere prayer life, faithfully reading God's Word, applying His truth and principles to our everyday life, and having a receptive spirit to the work of the Holy Spirit within us. These characterize our journey. This takes discipline and perseverance, dedication and commitment, and a hunger to be a follower of Christ and a vessel of honor. **"Work out your own salvation in reverence and awe"** (Ph. 2:12).

Paul writes to the Believers at Ephesus: "*Therefore, my dear ones, as you have always obeyed (my suggestions), so now, not only (with the enthusiasm you would show) in my presence but much more because I am absent, work out (cultivate, carry you to the goal and fully complete) your own salvation with reverence and awe and trembling (self-distrust, that is, with serious caution, tenderness of conscience, watchfulness against temptation; timidly shrinking from whatever might offend God and discredit the name of Christ. Not in your own strength) for it is God Who is all the while effectively at work in you (energizing and creating in you the power and desire) both to will and to work for His good pleasure and satisfaction and delight*" (Ph. 2:12-13) (Amp.Ver.).

In our spiritual development, we yield to His control, He enlarges our vision, establishes us in our faith, and effectively uses us for His glory. He will lead us in every venture (Prov. 3:5-6). He enables us to **"*work out your own salvation in reverence and awe.*"**

There is no short cut to spiritual maturity. Our life and character are the outward displays of the *in-living Christ*. God implants His righteousness in us as a *new creation in Christ*. It is evident in the Believer who has been "*renewed in the spirit of his mind,*" whose motives, thoughts, attitudes and priorities are founded in God alone. This should be the "*most reasonable thing we can do*" (Rom. 12:1-2). The faithfulness of our walk and dedication of our life to God should be obvious to what has taken place in our hearts and manifested in our life by the power of God.

God wants to embrace our life with His Life ... our longing with His Fullness ... our neglect with His Faithfulness ... our ineffectiveness with His Mighty Power ... our weakness with His Strength! We should not question God nor challenge the validity of His Sovereignty. We are to have unwavering faith in His constant care, His unfailing concern, His loving compassion, and His unerring faithfulness. See Lam. 3:22-23.

Let God cleanse and renew, reconcile and restore, fill and overflow our heart in a glorious intimate relationship with our blessed Savior Jesus Christ.

> **It is not *what we do* but *what we believe*. It is not *who we are* but *Who He is*. "Work out your own salvation in reverence and awe."**

An Amazing Design

Many of us live too much in the *"fast lane"* to see the marvels and miracles of our Supernatural God. Everywhere we look we can see the *footprints of God* in His miraculous designs that are inconceivable and beyond our comprehension.

On a business trip to India, I had the opportunity to visit a family business that wove beautiful handmade oriental rugs. I was fascinated to see, firsthand, the intricacy of the design, how it was done, and the skillful young hands that produced such a *"marvel of workmanship."* Because of the demand placed upon these workers in weaving the special thread and tying unending knots on the underside ... most of the work is limited to young people. The weaver's hands become, coarse, stiff, and difficult to manage after several years, and they have to abandon their work. On average, a skilled weaver can only make three 9 foot x 12 foot rugs a year.

The design is produced from the underside, sometimes with bright light shining on the specific area they are working on. It takes unusual patience, perseverance, and strong skilled hands to accomplish such a demanding project. The joy becomes unreal when the rug is complete and is turned over to reveal its _amazing design_ to the untiring worker. He beams with great satisfaction. You stand in awe of such a monumental task of weaving a true oriental rug.

I thought of the infinite designs God has produced. His _most amazing design_ is the radical transformation of an unbeliever: one without God, without hope, and, by his own choice, separated eternally from God and bound for eternal condemnation. When God transforms his life, it is *a miracle of the Supernatural Grace of God.* His <u>amazing design</u> and task features a *"one-of-a-kind"* work that *only God could do.*

God takes us through varied experiences, designing our life with minute care and color to perfect His plan and purpose. We experience the dark colors of distress, adversity and devastation that give us *depth of character.* The bright colors contrasted with the dark ones highlight the *beauty of His Presence and Power.* The dreary and wearisome colors subtly compliment the dark and bright ones and bring together *completeness* to the intricate overall design by God Himself. It reveals His infinite love, grace, and mercy.

Often, we recall experiences that were devastating at the time. We wondered how He could include such an occasion and make it turn out to His glory. Through submission to His will, His amazing design comes together ... *through His Divine Hand upon our life ...* that reflects the longsuffering and love He has taken to perfect His predestined plan.

We begin to understand Rom. 8:28-29 (Amp.Ver.):

"And we are assured and know that **ALL things work together** *and are (fitting into a plan) for good to those who love God and are called according to* **(His) design and purpose ... to be molded into the image of His Son."**

His <u>amazing design</u> is a *"work-in-progress."* He challenges us to look beyond what is visible to the invisible ... from what we can grasp to that which exceeds our capabilities ... from the finite boundaries of man to the infinite resources of God. *His design* always looks beyond what is impossible to man but possible with God.

In His grace, His ever-loving hands weave an amazing design of His purpose and plan in our life. May we be submissive to the intricate workings of God ... to perfect the Design of His Choice ... for His glory ... by the Master Weaver. We can never attain what only God can design. Embrace it and live in the wonder of it all!

Lord, I'm Returning Home

These are words that rejoice the hearts of parents of a loved one who has been traveling down the wrong road and has been awakened to his need, returning to a godly home where forgiveness, compassion, care and comfort will impact that need with embraces of love. To leave such a blessed place to do "*our thing*" and explore what an alluring but superficial world has to offer is a downward path that will cost us a great price. **Lord, I'm returning home!**

How attractive and exciting it is when we think, *"Now I am free!* I can do what I want to do, go where I want to go and make <u>my choices</u> without the influence of my parents and friends." The road <u>seemed</u> paved with opportunity, money, success, and abundant freedom from which I could choose. Friends came easy as they influenced me to compromise my faith in order to follow them in their carnal and sinful pursuits. Those times didn't seem harmful or challenging to what I had been taught by my parents from His Word. I was being deceived by Satan himself.

I continued down this illusive, costly path until I realized the bright lights and unrealistic charm had a faulty foundation that was beginning to undermine the ingrained values I had been taught as I was growing up. I was sacrificing it all and yielding my life to the infiltrating ways of the arch deceiver, Satan himself. That which I longed for was fast fading away. This was <u>not the freedom</u> I expected when I left home. This was *not the peace or reality of life* I had heard about and been taught. Every pursuit, even when accomplished, was but a *deceptive realization* of what I expected. I realized the <u>*friends*</u> were using me to further their gain, not mine. **Lord, I'm returning home!**

When I made that decision, I knew there would be much to confess and repent of. I had been unfaithful to the Lord and those who loved me most. I had been motivated by a self-centered mindset, consumed with pride and an egotistical, arrogant attitude. Satan and his adversaries had invaded me as they, unknowing to me, infiltrated my life and caused me to pursue a lifestyle that took me down a lonely self-centered road in every way. *Only the infinite grace of God can avail to forgive, redeem and bring back man to the life God created him for.* **Lord, I'm returning home!**

How unworthy and defeated I felt. I realized what a mess I had made of my life! I remember that my Mother taught me a verse that was now so suitable for me: *"If we confess our sins, He is faithful and just to forgive us our sins and to cleanse us from all unrighteousness"* (1 John 1:9).

What would it be like to be forgiven, set free, and know *His joy* that is unspeakable and full of glory, *His peace* that passes human understanding, and *be reconciled* to God, my family and friends, who truly loved me? My heart began to well up in anticipation; tears began to stream down my face as I thought with increasing humility of being in that blessed place I call *home*. **Lord, I'm returning home!**

Unbelievable love abounded; reconciliation and forgiveness was freely expressed *when I returned home*. I was overwhelmed to be received again where the reality of God's Presence was a part of my *"walk with the Lord each day."* Home at last, **I was unshackled** from my past sin and bondage ... **to freedom, peace, and hope! Praise the Lord**!

God will take the broken pieces of our life and make something beautiful out of them when they are surrendered to His loving care. **Lord, I'm returning home.**

The Well Is Deep

We are bewildered many times by our limited human understanding and reasoning. We often confine them within the boundaries of <u>our</u> capabilities, leaving God out of the difficulty we confront. This is especially true when we live spiritually on the *circumference* of God's Might and Power rather than in the *center,* where all the action is, *close to the heart of God.*

When Jesus asked the woman of Samaria, *"Give me to drink,"* she responded with great consternation. She didn't realize to Whom she was talking. She said, *"Sir, thou hast nothing to draw with, and* **the well is deep:** *from whence then hast thou that living water?"* ... *Then Jesus replied, "Whosoever drinketh of the water that I shall give him shall never thirst; but the water that I shall give him shall be in him a well of water springing up into everlasting life"* (John 4:11-14).

There are deep <u>weights of doubt</u> within our heart that hinders God from extending His helpful hand. *Doubt rules out God* and focuses on *our need and <u>our</u> ability* to meet that need. God says, **"Come unto Me** *all ye that labor and are heavy laden, and I will give you rest"* (Matt. 11:28). We respond, "But Lord, my burden is too heavy, I cannot draw from the life-giving waters the strength, comfort and peace I desperately need ... **the well is deep.**"

God withholds His mighty power... when we purposely rely on our finite resources and live within our self-imposed boundaries. God never meets our need from drawing from human nature ... *our help cometh from above.* "But my God shall supply ALL your need **according to His riches**

in glory by Christ Jesus" (Phil. 4:19). Paul said, *"I can do all things through Christ who strengthens me"* (Phil. 4:14).

Doubt is but one of the many weights within our heart that hinder His work of grace and needs to be addressed. We are encumbered with the weights of fear, aggravation, frustration, anger, resentment, anxiety, apprehension, an unforgiving spirit, and a host of other concerns that discourage, defeat, and destroy our child-like faith in our Almighty God.

The well is deep ... but there is no depth that He cannot fathom or need He cannot meet. There is nothing too small that He will fail to see and deal with in care and compassion ... or anything too great that His mighty power cannot conquer. When we focus on the *greatness of our Almighty God* ... all these <u>*deep weights within*</u> lose their finite significance in the light of His Omnipotent Presence. Nothing lies beyond implicit, unwavering faith in Almighty God except that which lies outside His will.

Faith knows no bounds or staggers at the promises of God or the declarations of His grace. Faith reaches out to the unknown, the unseen, the unimaginable, and claims the impossible.

When we are overcome with trouble, He is *our Stronghold* (Ps. 27:1) ... Whenever we are in want, He is *our Shepherd* (Ps. 23:1) ... In the night seasons, *"He is a lamp unto our feet and a light unto our path"* (Ps. 118:105) ... In sickness, *He is the Lord that heals and comforts* (Ps. 103:3 and Ex. 15:26). ... When we face devastating adversity, *He is my Conqueror* (Rom. 8:35-37) ... When in doubt and distress, *He is my incomparable Christ* (Rom. 8:38-39).

The well is deep. *In His Grace He enables us to plumb its depths and* ***draw from the life-giving, everlasting springs of God to re-establish our life ... by His grace, in His strength, for His glory!***

My Perspective

Your _perspective of life_ determines your decisions, interests, activities, and friends. It is an attitude and concern we need to seriously consider. First, we must decide what is our *"point of reference."* It will determine the *perspective* from which we look at life.

To most, their *perspective of life* is that of the world ... with its alluring attractions, money, power, and influence that strongly persuades us to pursue its superficial goals. Such a *point of view* centers in self-attainment, selfish gains, and self-independence ... encouraged by having _self_ control our life. Worldly cares, the deceitfulness of its riches, attractions, and the lusts of the flesh obstruct all that God has put in us.

Sadly, after we have exhausted our efforts to attain our goals, we find we have been disillusioned. The exhilaration and satisfaction we expected eludes us. Our accomplishment only drives us on to pursue even more goals. The joy, peace, satisfaction, and contentment we desire will only be realized when our endeavors have a *"sure foundation."* **A worldly _perspective_ has a volatile and precarious foundation.**

How does the Christian _perspective_ differ from that of the unbeliever? First, the Believer has, as his *"point of reference,"* the truth: principles and precepts of God's Word ... the validity and character of God, and the indwelling presence and power of the Holy Spirit to formulate his *godly point of view.* He brings every thought and imagination into captivity to the obedience of Christ. His interests, concerns, and viewpoint reach their highest point when their attitude of mind, heart and body is focused on Jesus Christ as the *priority of their life*. They are not looking for the *benefits* of knowing Christ ... but rather of **knowing Him.**

Matthew wrote a simple but profound truth that should challenge every Believer to unwavering trust in God in every phase of their life: *"If God so clothe the grass of the field ... shall he not **much more clothe you?**"* (Matt. 6:30). We so often say in our self-assurance, "*God is not interested* in the details of my business, personal relationships, concerns, and circumstances." **Oh, but He is.** That's where *we fail so miserably* in our walk with the Lord!

When our *perspective of life* has *Jesus Christ as the Lord and Authority of ALL of our life* ... we begin to see things done in and through our life that **only God could have done!** *This is part of our exciting journey through life.* It begins with having our *"point of reference"* in Christ alone ... opening up our heart to His leading and work of grace.

When you look at Paul, you realize he was not devoted to a *cause* but to *the Person of Jesus Christ.* He was brought into a personal overmastering relationship to HIM. His whole *perspective of life* centered in **knowing Christ.** His testimony was, *"But what things were gain to me, those I counted loss for Christ. I count all things but loss for the excellency of the knowledge of Christ Jesus my Lord: for whom I have suffered the loss of all things, and do count them as dung, that I may win Christ ... **that I may know Him**"* (Phil. 3: 7- 10).

His new *perspective of life* radically changed his life. God withholds His mighty power ... when we purposively live within our self-imposed boundaries, forced upon us by having a worldly perspective of life! *To plunder in the way of our selfish will is sure defeat. To surrender our will to His Lordship is a sure and awesome victory!* **When we focus our heart on the Majesty of God, His will, and His way ... everything else loses its finite significance.**

The Temple Of The Holy Ghost

When the children of Israel started their forty year wilderness journey, God called Moses aside and told him to build *The Tabernacle*. It was God's Dwelling Place among them. It was evidence of His abiding presence and power, and of His covenant with them.

The *"cloud by day and the fire by night"* was His means of guiding them when and where they should go. If an Israelite had any doubts, fear, or alarm, they had only to *look up* and see either the cloud by day or fire by night and be assured that God was with them and would provide their every need to them. God's presence was in the Holy of Holies.

After being born again by God's supernatural grace, Paul addresses the Believers at Corinth, *"What? know you not **that your body is the temple of the Holy Ghost** which is in you, which you have of God, and you are not your own? For you have been bought with a price: **therefore glorify God in your body, and in your spirit, which are God's"*** (1 Cor. 6:19-20).

Our salvation is eternally secure. His grace is greater than all our sin ... His mercy is everlasting ... and His infinite love is beyond measure. Paul writes about our daily walk and how we should respond as being *"in Christ."* He challenges us to *work out what God has worked in*. We are responsible to manifest in our body the life of the Lord Jesus.

We have been made a *"new creature in Christ"* (2 Cor. 5:17). Our body is now **"the temple of the Holy Ghost,"** *something that has not been present before.* Our body, in which the Holy Spirit abides, becomes a living reality of His presence and power. His life flows through us freely when **we will** to Him *"our right and authority"* to govern our life.

Paul challenges us, *"Do not conform any longer to the pattern of this world, but **be you transformed by the renewing of your mind.** Then you will be able to test and approve what God's will is ... His good, pleasing and perfect will"* (Rom. 12:1-2)(NIV).

"His divine power hath given unto us all things that pertain unto life and godliness, *through the knowledge of Him that has called us to glory and virtue: whereby are given unto us exceeding great and precious promises: that **by these you might be partakers of the divine nature"*** (2 Peter 1:3-4).

Paul not only challenges us what we need to do but also how we can enter into a *covenant relationship with Him.* The only thing God wants of us is *our unconditional surrender.* We do not question, debate, or contest His demands of discipleship, which come from His infinite love. We must respond in simple but profound *trust in God.* His blessings are no longer the ultimate desire of our heart, but rather, we want an *intimate personal relationship with Him.* We covet the *"Living Water"* to flow fully from our innermost being.

It is the Believers privilege *"making God Himself his habitual dwelling"* (Ps. 91:9). *It is His life* flowing through *"the temple of the Holy Spirit,"* **our body.** Only when we have experienced this blessed privilege do we know the indescribable communion between God and our spirit. This is a mercy only the true Believer enjoys. *May we manifest in all of our life the purity of our intentions, the simplicity of our minds and the integrity of our heart that will glorify the Lord.* **We are the temple of the Holy Ghost!**

"Therefore, I urge you, brothers, in view of God's mercy, to offer your bodies as living sacrifices, holy and pleasing to God ... this is your spiritual act of worship" (Rom. 12:1).

A Father's Love

God will not impose Himself upon us; neither will He insist on being the Authority of our life. He will not coerce, force, or compel us to follow Him. He has given to us a *"free will"* to answer *the standards of discipleship.* **We choose and we will** to answer His challenge. Jesus does not demand obedience; *He sets the standard* and it is up to us to accept or reject it. Jesus said, *"If any man will come after me, let him deny himself, and take up his cross daily and follow me"* (Luke 9:23). **The prerequisite is always on us, not God.**

Our relationship with God is not that of a robot under His control but rather that of *a father and son.* We respond out of love to God our Father, indebtedness to all He is and has done for us, and are overwhelmed with His giving of Himself to us that we may be molded in a life that will honor and glorify Him. His infinite love, manifested to us, has secured our unwavering trust in Him. We live in obedience to Him, not by constraint but by the exercise of a heart of love to answer His desires fully.

When I thought along these principles, I was reminded of my earthly father. Ingrained in his character was a humble, self-giving spirit that never held back from doing whatever he could to influence my life to one of integrity, love, and grace. I saw in him one who exercised a quiet spirit-filled life with love that overwhelmed me with his grace, that won my unending love and devotion. My love for my earthly father was not the result of a demanding personality but, rather, a spirit of trust and an eagerness to be one in unity, spirit, and faithfulness. My obedience was not *"worked up, debated, or considered"* ... it was *"natural."* Even more, it was my privilege and my earnest desire to be all he wanted me to be ... to reflect the integrity and honor he deserved.

All of these virtues of a loving earthly father are but a minute reflection of the infinite love of God to us, His children. His relationship to us is that of a father and his children. God laid down principles of conduct for those who have been redeemed. Calvary displayed the infinite love of God and the total obedience of His Son, Jesus Christ paying the debt of our sin.

Standing at the foot of the Cross, we behold the Lamb of God in all His godly virtues as He took upon Himself the sin of the whole world. He cries out to the Father, *"My God, my God, why hast thou forsaken me?"* (Matt. 27: 46). When God had accepted His sacrifice for our sin, Jesus cries out, *"It is finished"* (John 19:30). Our salvation was complete, the price had been paid, and God's love was manifested before the world through His grace ... that's greater than all our sin!

The attitude of our life should be one of obedience to Him ... of complete devotion and commitment to His will and purpose for our life. It is the *"unworthiness"* in us that refuses to bow down to the *"Worthy One"* in unconditional surrender. In humility and contrition, we come before Him.

True obedience comes from the *"heart of God."* Such obedience makes a radical difference in the way we live, the degree of our commitment, the dedication of our lives, the manner of our worship, the faithfulness of our prayer life, the consistency of our service, and the steadfastness of our testimony.

> ***True obedience is paramount and indispensable to our faith and our life before the Holy and Just One ... to the Father's love given on Calvary's Cross for you and me.***

Thou Art The Man

David's dreadful fall began when we read, *"But David tarried still at Jerusalem"* (2 Sam. 11:1). He remained, but sent his soldiers into battle rather than being with them as they fought the enemy. Secondly, *"As he walked on the roof of the king's house: and from the roof he saw a beautiful woman washing herself; and the woman was very beautiful to look upon"* (vs. 2). The *lusts of the flesh* overcame his righteous judgment when he saw Bathsheba. David began to orchestrate an ungodly plan to have her ... even the murder of Uriah, her husband. He carried out his plan. Uriah was killed in battle, and David took Bathsheba as his wife.

Afterward, God sent Nathan to appear before David who told him the parable of the rich man and the poor man: *"David's anger was greatly kindled"* (2 Sam. 12:5). David thought what an immeasurable injustice had been done by the rich man. David then proclaimed what should be done to the rich unjust man. Then Nathan said, **"Thou art the man."**

What a sad account of this mighty King of Israel. His life was never the same after this disclosure and the judgment of God upon him. His heart was broken; the glory of being the greatest King Israel had ever known was taken from him by the betrayal of his own son, Absalom. Many were the sorrows David incurred after this sad occasion.

One insightful thought prevailed when Nathan told him, *"Thou art the man."* David realized to Whom he belonged and confessed, **"Against thee, and thee only, have I sinned, and done this evil in thy** *sight"* (Ps. 51:4). When he confessed his sin, God forgave him, but *David bore the scars of his sin the rest of his life.* It was not his relationship with men that concerned him the greatest ... *but* **his relationship with God**.

Why do you think we, as Believers, have such *an attitude of permissiveness* that encourages freedom for expressing our liberal tolerance with sin? First, **we have lost our vision of the Majesty of God** ... His Holiness, Righteousness and Justice. God is not the priority of our life and does not reign as the Sovereign Authority on the throne of our heart. Secondly, we feel **"we have the right to rule our life** ... *to exercise our natural independence and self-assertiveness."* Therefore, we open the door of our life to Satan and his seducing evil influence. These were David's thoughts as he looked upon Bathsheba: it resulted in his dreadful fall.

In the measure we revere the holiness of God, so will be the measure of our response, our reverence, our worship and our commitment to Him. The worth of a Believer is found in his daily walk in ordinary things. It's not when he is acclaimed or honored but when found among commonplace circumstances. *God desires to put His truth into the minds of those who follow Him, His Compassion in their hearts, His Will into their lives, and make His Lordship Sovereign.*

Our **spiritual stature** *and maturity* is learned from a discerning spirit, which the Holy Spirit gives unto us, not by intellectual reasoning. *Our* **character** is developed and made strong as we discipline ourselves to *"abide in Christ."* God is concerned with the **<u>attitude</u>** *that affects how we live ... the* **<u>motive</u>** *that underlies the things we do ... the* **<u>principles</u>** *that mold our lives ... the* **<u>priorities</u>** *that determine our decisions ... the* **<u>love</u>** *that abounds in our hearts and reflects our commitment.*

May the truth and principles we have mentioned above so adorn our walk that others will be convinced of the dedication of our life to Christ. **"Now by this I know that thou art a man of God"** (1 Kings 17: 24).

"Jesus Took A Towel"

(John 13:5)

The virtues of Christ leave us in a state of consternation and dismay. We cannot fathom the quiet humble spirit He manifested ... the grace He displayed as He moved among the cross-grain of humanity. We marvel at the path He chose, reaching out to the poor, the sick, the needy, the outcasts of society with compassion and love. **"Jesus took a towel ... and began to wash the disciples' feet"** (John 13:5).

This act of humility was for the lowest servant, which the disciples would not bend down to do. Yet, here is Jesus, their Lord and Master, taking the lowest part of the lowest servant. His words to His disciples, *"You call Me Master and Lord: and you say well; for so I am. If I then, your Lord and Master, have washed your feet; you also ought to wash one another's feet.* **For I have given you an example, that you should do as I have done to you"** (John 13:13-15).

Where do we find ourselves amidst a scene as this? Unfortunately, in our Christian walk we look for the *big things* ... to be seen, recognized, and applauded by man. Jesus walked among the lowly, the beggars and the abandoned that He might minister unto them the *refreshing, life-giving waters that never run dry.* Jesus also confounded the proud, the intelligent, and the rulers of His day by *His masterful display of mercy and grace.*

Paul's challenge, **"Let this mind be in you, which was also in Christ Jesus:** *Who, being in the form of God, thought it not robbery to be equal with*

God: But made himself of no reputation, and **took upon Him the form of a servant,** *and was made in the likeness of men: And being found in fashion as a man, he humbled himself, and became obedient unto death, even the death of the cross"* (Phil. 2:5-8). **"Jesus took a towel ... and began to wash the disciples' feet."**

We look at our service as what *"we do for Him"* ... whereas Jesus looks at *"what we are to Him."* Discipleship is not dependent upon creedal adherence but on our commitment and devotion to Jesus Christ as our Lord and Sovereign Authority. Today, we find so much emphasis devoted to <u>a cause, a need, or a project</u> rather than *unreservedly being focused on Jesus Christ*. When He is the Lord of our life, the work of the ministry and its vision will find their particular place. He must be first and foremost in our life. *Let this mind be in you that was also in Christ Jesus* ... **"Jesus took a towel ... and began to wash the disciples' feet."**

When we entrust childlike faith in our Almighty God, He opens our eyes to His unfathomable Majesty and **we stand in awe of All He Is.** God enlarges our heart of devotion, deepens our faith, and draws us into an intimate personal relationship with Him. He becomes *unspeakably precious and is the consuming desire of our hearts and the passion of our journey.*

A radical *renovation of our heart* is not reformation but a glorious transformation wrought by the power of Almighty God. We turn from self-independence and focus our heart on Him, that we might please the Father and be clothed with His humility and grace. *May we seek to walk as He walked* (John 2:6) ... *Love as He loved* (Eph. 3:17- 19) ... *Be holy as He is holy* (1 Peter 1:16).

This is an exciting venture of faith that finds its fulfillment by walking in obedience to His commands, surrendering our life to the Lordship of Christ, and doing the will of God. **"Jesus took a towel ... and began to wash the disciples' feet."**

Why Reconciliation?

Why do Believers insist on a self-centered, self-independent attitude in their heart? To condone a *"contrary spirit"* will devastate, destroy, and contribute to our isolation from God and others. It is detrimental to all of our relationships. We will be the one most negatively affected. Our efforts to live for God will be but *"hay, wood and stubble."*

First, such an attitude finds its roots deep within the heart where <u>self</u> reigns. Sadly, we do not recognize the *"sin within"* because of the deceitfulness of our own heart ... or we purposely yield to Satan's illusion that we are <u>right</u> and everybody else is <u>wrong</u>. The standard we are living by, making observations and judgments, are **"not God's standard" ... but our own.** Satan has *cunningly infiltrated our life* that we do not recognize who is in control. This causes devastating grief, misunderstanding, heartache, false accusations, and great detriment to all concerned.

Secondly, when we have a <u>self-independent</u> attitude we are motivated by *"our selfish will"* ... not under the control of the Holy Spirit. **We think we know best** and can handle every issue we face. Our relationship with the Lord is *"at our convenience."* Consequently, He is not the priority of our life. **We do not feel our daily need of God or our dependence on Him when we exercise our self-independent attitude.**

We say, *"This is not true in my life."* Then, why the strife, anger, unforgiving spirit, accusations, untruth, and selfish manifestations *so evident to those who you feel have offended you?* **What is the answer?** If we are sincere in wanting the Lord to live in and through us, listen to what God says in Matt. 5:23-24: "... ***first be reconciled to your brother.***" This is the beginning of reconciliation. Oswald Chambers writes clearly and profoundly ... *"Sin is a fundamental relationship; it is not wrong doing, it is **wrong being ... deliberate, emphatic, self-independence of God.**"* When we have an unforgiving spirit, we refrain from addressing sin in ourselves and ignore what God wants to do in our life to cleanse us from all iniquity and create within our hearts a clean spirit and pure heart (Ps. 51: 7-10). Until we humble ourselves, confess our sin, and repent ... we will continue to be unreceptive to the leading of the Holy Spirit and *manifest a self-independent attitude that is deplorable to God.* That's why reconciliation is imperative.

What is reconciliation? It is restoring mutual respect, re-establishing normal relations, being accountable for our behavior, returning to the faith that honors God after a conflict, and *bringing back mutual trust, admiration, and confidence in the character of the one who has offended us.*

What do we need to remember? Jesus said, *"For if you forgive not men their trespasses, neither will your Father forgive your trespasses"* (Matt. 7:15). *"Judge not, that you be not judged. For with what judgment you judge, you shall be judged ..."* (Matt. 7:1). When the Pharisees and scribes brought to Jesus the women caught in adultery and tempted Him regarding what the law said, He turned to them and said, *"He that is without sin among you, let him first cast a stone at her"* (John 8:9). **Are we above these penetrating words of Jesus? Not in any sense.**

When we face verbal abuse *and anger, it is an opportunity for us to respond in His grace and manifest the reality of our faith in Christ.* This is *"His supernatural life"* being lived through us. Grace is giving to another what they do not deserve and *"standing tall"* in the power of God. **When the Lord is in control of our life, we reflect His grace and love. A critical, judging, unforgiving spirit vanishes. HE reigns.**

The Discipline Of Obedience

We are so prone to interpret God's providential care according to <u>our</u> understanding, thus, interfering with His permissive will for us. We are designed with a great capacity for God; but, when our individuality and sin prevail, *we inhibit God* from His work of grace and the development of our spiritual life of obedience. God will not impose or force His will on us. Our free will is responsible to surrender our individual rights, relinquish our self-centered will to His divine control, and allow Him to rule and reign as Sovereign in our life. This gives the Holy Spirit freedom to work in us to where we are invaded by the very *nature of God*.

The *discipline of obedience* brings us into the highest level of introspection and enables us to see *Who God Is!* Abraham recognized *Who God Is* and in **abandoned obedience to Him** was ready to sacrifice Isaac, his only son and the son of promise, until God withheld his hand and provided a ram.

Job saw *Who God Is.* After all of his suffering and trials, he saw God in the magnitude of His Majesty. Then he saw himself as God saw him and said, *"I have heard thee by the hearing of the ear: but now mine eye seeth thee. Wherefore I abhor myself, and repent in dust and ashes"* (Job 42: 5-6).

Isaiah knew *Who God Is*, *"I saw the Lord sitting upon a throne, high and lifted up, and his train filled the temple ... Then said I, Woe is me! For I am undone; because I am a man of unclean lips ... **for mine eyes have seen the King, the Lord of host"*** (Isa. 6:1,5). With these godly men, we also, will bow humbly at His feet and respond in deep contrition and repentance when we **"See the King!"** Jesus Christ wants our *absolute* *abandon of devotion to Himself* and reign as Lord and Sovereign of our life!

Obedience opens unto us the *nature of God* and we begin to understand the depths and passion of His promises as we *"partake of the divine nature"* (2 Peter 1:4). The promises of God become precious and affective when the *nature of God embraces all of our life.* Knowing <u>Who God Is</u> initiates the first step of living within the *discipline of obedience.*

Anything that is not based on our personal relationship to God competes with and hinders the *discipline of obedience* to God. His concern is that we trust and depend on Him and His power <u>now</u>. God trains us <u>now</u> ... manifests His power <u>now</u> ... disciplines us <u>now</u>. It is our responsibility to <u>obey now</u>. It is His responsibility to *bring in the harvest.* **We have nothing to do with the results of obedience; we have everything to do with being obedient.**

God wants us to be in the center of His will, not concerned with peripheral endeavors. His way is simple yet profound ... we make it difficult and confusing. Ask God for spiritual discernment that we might know the *"mind of Christ"* in all of our endeavors. *True obedience is paramount and indispensable to our faith.*

We have trouble rationalizing the *discipline of obedience* to our liking, rather than recognizing and submitting to the authority of His Word. If we expect God's Hand upon our life, there can be no deviation from His commands to *walk in obedience* and live under the Authority of His Lordship. *"If it seem evil unto you to serve the Lord, choose you this day whom you will serve, but as for me and my house, we will serve the Lord"* (Joshua 24:15). **Love leads us to unwavering obedience. Obedience opens the floodgates of God's presence and power in our lives.**

Fear

It is amazing how often we are encumbered with this destructive characteristic that breaks down our confidence, undermines our faith, and devastates our best efforts. When we try to confront and deal with *fear* in *our own capabilities*, it often grips our very being, destroys, discourages, and defeats us. God's Word says, *"Greater is HE that is in you than he that is in the world"* (1 John 4:4).

When we allow *fear* to control our hearts, emotions, and mind, we are focusing on our circumstances rather than the might and power of God. Our circumstances come between God and us. We turn from all He has given to us and purchased for us and allow this dreadful issue to disrupt our focus on God. Such action obliterates our trust in the Omnipotent One, who will enable us to *confront fear in the power of God and triumph over it.*

Fear is a distressing emotion aroused by impending evil, pain, distress, apprehension, dismay, uncertainty, rejection, and many other situations that we encounter from day to day. *Fear,* when left alone, will restrain us from surrendering our need to *His control.* We turn from casting this devastating need on Christ and try to overcome *fear* in the confines of our own futile and finite understanding,

God said, *"Fear thou not; for **I am with you**: be not dismayed; for **I am your God**: I will **strengthen you**; yea, I will **help you**; yea, I will **uphold you** with the right hand of my righteousness"* (Isaiah 41: 10). This is God's irrevocable promise to every Believer that will **"dare to Believe and Trust Him!"** Let these words penetrate our heart and establish unwavering confidence and faith in Our Almighty God *"Who will lift us up from our despair to the conquering heights by His mighty power."*

Why are we so reluctant to cast <u>*fear*</u> into the Hands of the One who has promised to deliver us from this oppression? Basically, **because we do not believe His promise nor do we expect it to be fulfilled!** This is blatant unbelief and rejection of God and His grace. We are saying, *"Our fear is greater than God!"* O, we respond, "I wouldn't say that." Then why do we refrain from trusting Him to deliver us from this bondage of fear? We sulk in our incompetence, complain in our inability to overcome our fear, and continue to be discouraged, overcome, and defeated.

What is the answer for the Believer? Where there is unerring wisdom to direct and deliver, God's almighty power to execute His plan, a receptive spirit to follow His leading, <u>*fear*</u>, with all of its demeaning ways, cannot overcome *His infinite grace to set us free and deliver us from its bondage.*

Yielding to <u>*fear*</u> is always a <u>*downward*</u> journey; we go down from high and holy fellowship with God ... down from dedicated service and self-restraint, and down from an intimate relationship with the Lord. <u>*Fear*</u> hardens our heart, stupefies our conscience, and causes us to be concerned only with the burden and anxieties *we allow* to encompass us. **Trust in God, HE is our Great Deliverer!**

I have guilt that nothing but the blood of Christ can wash away. I have corruption and fear that none but the Holy Spirit can subdue and mortify. I have wants that nothing but an All-Sufficient Savior can supply.

Having Christ as my Savior, Refuge, Strength, Righteousness, Daily Companion, Security, and My All ... I HAVE NOTHING TO FEAR ... He conquered our dilemma at Calvary!

God's Refreshing Waters

Have you ever had the experience of drinking from a clear, cool, refreshing spring? Hot and thirsty, dehydrated and drained, you drank from a spring that finds its source and origin at the <u>Fountainhead</u>. What an invigorating and energizing experience. Through the cleansing process of God, He filters the contamination and impurities from these waters and makes them pure, refreshing, and satisfying to all.

Jesus said unto the women of Samaria, *"If you knew the gift of God, and who it is that says to you, Give me to drink; you would have asked of him, and he would have given you living water ... Whosoever drinks of this water shall thirst again: but whosoever drinks of the water that I shall give him shall never thirst; but* **the water that I will give him shall be in him a well of water springing up into everlasting life"** (John 4:10,14).

Jesus is the <u>Fountainhead</u> from which these *"rivers of living waters"* are initiated. He is not the channel, but the Mighty Source. These refreshing waters are persistent, continuously flowing, and give unto us a victorious and an irrepressible life! He says, *"From our innermost being shall flow rivers of living water"* (John 7:38).

Have you ever seen the mighty force of floodwaters that have been channeled into a defying, unrelenting torrent of destruction? Such are the life-giving waters of God when we have *abandoned trust in Him*. When obstacles of difficulty, trials and devastating experiences confront us, He either takes us *"victoriously through the difficulty or makes a path around it."* The Spirit of God, with "His rivers of living waters," overcomes all obstacles. Read Isaiah 43:1-3:

"For no temptation has overtaken you and laid hold on you that is not common to man – that is, no temptation or trial has come to you that is beyond human resistance and that is not adjusted and adapted and belonging to human experience, and such as man can bear. **But God is faithful** (to His Word and compassionate nature), *and He* (can be trusted) *will not let you be tempted and tried beyond your ability* and strength of resistance and power to endure, *but will with the temptation or trial, He will (always) also provide the way out*–the means of escape to a landing place-*that you may be capable* and strong and powerfully patient *to bear up under it"* (1 Cor. 10:13) (Amp. Ver.).

How blessed to live in the reality of having the *"rivers of living waters"* flowing through us in refreshing and life-giving virtues to others. So many lives are thirsting and parched from their drought of these spiritual waters. It is not a blessing to give to others, not a testimony of what we have experienced, but the living waters that originate with God as we resign our will to Him. It flows continuously from His *"well of water"* He has available to us (John 4:14). We must keep the channel clean and clear so these *"life-giving waters"* will flow unhindered, flowing full and free to others.

As we dare to believe and trust Him, <u>faith</u> reaches out to our Almighty God and He pours into our need His *"rivers of living waters."* We will come to Jesus as Comforter, Deliverer, and Refuge, but we have difficulty coming to Him as our **Almighty God ... the Omnipotent One**. *"My God is able to do exceeding abundantly above all we can ask or even think through His power that is at work in us"* (Eph. 3:20). **O that we might abandon ourselves to Jesus Christ and open the floodgates of His *"rivers of living waters."***

The Wonder Of His Presence

One of the wonders of God's grace is that He never forces His will or love upon us. He has made His grace, mercy, and love available to us ... *but on His terms.* He saves us by the virtue of His death on the Cross. *"For He (God) hath made Him (Jesus Christ) to be sin for us, who knew no sin; that we might be made the righteousness of God in Him"* (2 Cor. 5:21).

The certainty of God's presence is *real and active* when we place Him always before us as the priority of our life. It is the <u>reality</u> of His presence ... not simply the consciousness of His presence, and living with the assurance of His Word to us, *"Never will I leave you. Never will I forsake you"* (Heb. 13:5). How blessed to live day by day knowing and walking with Him as Friend, Companion, Lord, and Sovereign of our life! We follow Him in implicit obedience as His own.

How blessed is the <u>reality</u> *of your presence, Oh Lord!* Anytime, any place, in any situation, knowing the reality that You are there! Whether under sunny skies or times obscured by stormy clouds, while we are alarmed by the thunder and lightening ... *the joy of Your Presence is the strength of my life.* How blessed to walk with You, to hear your words of comfort, and assurance saying, *"This is the way, walk you in it, when you turn to the right hand, and when you turn to the left"* (Isa. 30:21).

There seems to be ingrained in our nature the attitude that *we must "do things"* in order to be accepted by God and others. We would rather *"work for God"* rather than undergird our life by *"trust in God."* The focus of our walk must be redirected from **all that**

*<u>we are</u> to all that <u>**He Is**</u>*. *Surrender finds its delight, significance, joy and fulfillment when accompanied by obedience in our life and walk.*

God must be the *Source and Strength* in all of our endeavors! The disciple of Christ is not characterized by an attitude of what we give up or by what we do or not do. It is rather, *"to throw off everything that hinders"* our devotion and commitment to God (Heb. 12:1,3) and be clothed with the virtues of Christ by His mighty power. It is then that we open up our life to all He wants to do in and through us.

God desires to give unto us a hundredfold for the wasted years of our life and fill them with present fruit, fervent endeavor and joyous reaping by the Holy Spirit. **God will take us from the ignominy of our past, to the blessing of the present, and the glory of the future.** As we dare to trust God, He unshackles the *"chains of iron"* that bind our life ... and transforms us to the praise of His glory and adorns us with the loveliness of Christ. *He reigns supreme!*

Oh the wonder of God's grace! We see *God's wisdom* and power in the works of His creation ... *His Goodness* demonstrated in the works of His Providence ... *His Grace* magnified in our redemption ... *His infinite love* manifested in the Atonement of Christ. *Blessed is the wonder of His presence!*

The victories of the past should be a springboard to launch us into greater avenues of faith and trust ... into larger areas of unchartered waters, that we might see His hand in the challenging encounters of our lives. From what we have received 'hitherto' we may claim by faith all that is 'henceforth.' *Dare to believe and trust Him completely.*

The Red Sea And Jericho

I am sure we can all recall a time when we were at our wit's end, and the only way out was up. We had *"hit bottom"* trying to confront our needs through <u>our</u> resources and strength. All human resources disappeared as we tried to grasp them for support and provision. We were lost in the darkness of the moment, exhausted by self-effort, and groped in a wilderness of distress and uncertainty.

As Israel faced the *Red Sea*, hemmed in by the mountains on both sides and the army of Pharaoh pursuing from behind, the *Red Sea* stood before them as a crushing vice. Humanly speaking, they faced sure defeat and annihilation. Where was their <u>*faith*</u> that trusted God in their miraculous exodus from their slavery and bondage in Egypt? *Was not Jehovah the same at the Red Sea as He was when He delivered them from Pharaoh's cruel enslavement?*

What happens when we face our *Red Sea?* To the Believer, he has the irrevocable promises of God to stand upon and claim by faith. *When we cannot see His Hand to lead us, we can trust His Heart to do what we cannot do and glorify Himself through it all.* **Venturesome, committed faith in God is bold, confident, trusting and courageous.** It takes God at His Word and believes, without delay or doubt, the truth that it is *"not by might, nor by power, but by My Spirit, saith the Lord"* (Zech. 4:6).

Moses said, **"Fear ye not, stand still, and see the salvation of the Lord,** *which He will show to you today: for the Egyptians whom you have seen today, you shall see them again no more forever.* **The Lord shall fight for you,** *and you shall hold your peace"* (Ex. 14:13-14). God parted the sea, *destroyed the enemy, and gave Israel a glorious victory!* How miraculous was the fall of *Jericho!* When Joshua saw the impenetrable walls that encircled the city, I'm sure, in the natural, he was in a state of severe consternation, especially when God gave him the <u>strange battle plan</u> to conquer this well-entrenched city. **Circumstances were no match to Joshua's unwavering faith in Almighty God. He dared to believe God against insurmountable circumstances!**

The formidable difficulties we encounter are limited by the measure that our hearts are engaged with the Omnipotent One. **They form no barrier to those whose heart is fixed on God.** God often allows devastating trials to come our way to test our faith, establish our walk, trust Him implicitly, and glorify Him through them. How true are the profound words of Martin Luther, **"If we would trust God, we must learn to crucify the question how."** Joshua's eyes were firmly fixed on God! Hear him say to his men, *"This is God's way. We will not question His wisdom but **firmly go forward in obedience and faith in His strength and power. He will give us the victory!**"* What characterizes our life when we face *our Red Sea* or the *impenetrable fortified Jericho?*

God watches over those who dare to trust Him. He restrains our adversaries (Ps. 4:6-7). *He comforts with His presence and power* (Isa. 43:1-3). *He imparts to us temporal and spiritual blessings (Matt. 6:33). He hears and answers our supplications* (John 15:7 and Jer. 33:3). *He communes with us as sons and daughters* (2 Cor. 6:18). *He takes upon Himself the management of our concerns* (Isa. 46:4) *as we dare to believe. How blessed to cast all our care on Him* (1 Peter 5:7). *To all who put their trust in Him, His presence and mighty power is the source of their richest consolation, the assurance of their trust, and the joy of their heart!*

Christ ... The Defining Issue

There are numerous views regarding Jesus Christ. He is regarded as a teacher, a moral example to follow, a symbol of respect, a righteous spiritual leader, or someone with personal meaningful characteristics to a particular person. **In truth, He is the defining issue of mankind.** Jesus Christ gave His life and shed His blood for our Atonement. He is the crux of mankind's relationship with God. To disregard His eternal significance is to refuse God's provision for mankind's sin to be reconciled to God through His love and grace.

It was on Calvary's Cross where Jesus Christ, the Son of God, paid the infinite ransom for the debt of our wretched sin. It is the shedding of His blood that cleanses us from all our sin. The Scriptures say, *"Almost all things are by the law purged with blood; and without the blood is no remission"* (Heb. 9:22). We are *justified* by his blood (Rom. 5:9), *redeemed* through his blood (Eph. 1:7), *made nigh* by the blood (Eph. 2:13), *have peace* through the blood of his Cross (Col. 1:20), and *cleansed* by the blood of Jesus (1 John 1:7). *"For He (God) hath made Him (Jesus) to be sin for us, who knew no sin; that we might be made the righteousness of God in Him"* (2 Cor. 5:21).

Jesus Christ is either the *bridge of redemption or the chasm of eternal condemnation.* Hell is prepared for Satan and his angels. We choose our eternal destination by either accepting God's way of salvation ... or *eternity in hell* by rejecting His love, spurning His grace, and turning our back on His mercy. The consequences of our sin hangs in the balance of our decision ... *What will you do with*

Jesus, who is called the Christ, the Son of God? Heaven is for all who receive Jesus Christ as their Lord and Savior. The choice is ours!

Jesus Christ stands before us when we are challenged to "*surrender our will*" to His Lordship and authority. We must decide whether to yield our life in *obedience to Jesus Christ and His word to us ...* or vindicate our own self-centered right to control our destiny. God will never force, impose, or compel our obedience. Our decision will determine our life here and in eternity. *Obedience* leads to the blessedness of His Presence, eternal security by His irrevocable covenant with us, and living in the strength and power as His child by his Atonement on Calvary.

Jesus Christ is the decisive issue we must face in our walk and fellowship with God. He will not condone sin or the compromise of our faith and commitment to Him. Simply "*professing faith in Christ without our works of obedience to His will*" is but the display of insincere effort on our part and an abomination to the Lord. We are trying to establish a walk with the Lord on *our terms*, not His. We want fellowship with the Holy One when *selfish interests and independence* are dominant and control our life, not Him.

It is not <u>the things we *do*</u> which are so often erroneously motivated but <u>what we believe</u> that determines *in Whom we trust*, how we walk, and opens up every phase of our life to His control and authority. *It is in Him, by Him, and through Him we walk in fellowship with God.* This is the only way we can experience an intimate personal relationship with Christ. Anytime we question or try to reason out by "*our understanding His truth*", we are on a downward spiritual spiral that separates us from blessed fellowship with Him. **Selfish-independence always has drastic ungodly consequences. His covenants** to us are irrevocable; **His blessings** are inconceivable; **His promises** are all inclusive, and **His power** gives to us freedom, peace, and hope ... and makes them a **reality in our lives!**

My Conversation With Jesus

Lord, I want to simply open my heart to You, bear my soul, and let you speak to me. You've blessed my life in immeasurable ways, many in which I am not even aware, through Your infinite grace. I thank You for these many ways. I'm also aware that Your Hand of grace has been on me in such an abounding way. *Thank You Lord!*

How trite it seems for me to simply, yet with all my heart, say *Thank You*. Yet, I know you understand my limitations in trying to say what I cannot put in words. As I look back over my life, you have been so gracious, even when I have been unfaithful, careless, and pursuing my way rather than Your way. You have been longsuffering and, in infinite love, forgiven me, lifted me up, and reestablished the intimacy of our walk together, when I was and am so undeserving of your grace. But that's just YOU!

I've rushed in "where angels have feared to tread." I've presumed upon Your mercy when I should have simply bowed humbly before You to know "the mind of Christ," Your plan and purpose. I've run full speed when I should have heeded the words of David: *"Wait on the Lord, be of good courage, and I will strengthen thine heart."* How selfish I've been all along the way, yet Your loving arms never failed to wrap themselves around me and say, *"I love you, trust ME, I'll show you the way and how to follow Me."*

Thank You Lord for being so understanding, forgiving, and merciful when I have been so out of touch with You, intent on doing my thing. I didn't realize how imperative it was to simply live each day in childlike faith in You. Forgive me for all these <u>self-centered</u>

attitudes and actions. I want to walk each day in the reality of my faith and in intimacy with You!

I'm sure You remember when I had that heart-wrenching experience as a Buyer for a large department store. I had my most successful year, yet when my review was given, I was literally <u>devastated</u> by a young man my age that had just been promoted to Merchandise Manager over our Division. For whatever reason, he *"wanted me out"* and made my review devastating. I was crushed, defeated, and felt utterly betrayed. I had worked diligently for years to achieve what *in a moment of time* was completely destroyed.

Lord, You know I was trusting You in those trying years, and when this happened, *I could not understand <u>why</u>.* You knew I had a family of three girls and my precious wife. I felt I had failed them and You miserably. Unbeknownst to me, **You had something far better,** and this crushing experience was necessary to get my heart <u>*focused on You*</u>. *In confession and repentance, I asked you to lead me to <u>higher ground</u> in Your time, Your way, and Your will.* You took my broken heart and made something beautiful out of it. *Thank You Jesus* for bringing me back to walk in the reality of my faith.

I resigned from that company, only to be offered a better position with their competitor. Five years later, You opened another door that was immeasurably better than these previous ones. *Looking back, I have seen how gracious, compassionate, and loving You were through all of this.* My faith was renewed and I started resting in You in a new and living way. *Thank You Lord* for *Your love* when I was so unlovely, *Your mercy* when I deserved Your judgment, and for *Your grace* that was more than I could ask for.

Now it's time again for me to listen to You, feel the warmth of Your presence, and hear You say, *"This is the way, walk you in it."* I stand in awe of All You Are! Speak Lord; your servant heareth and my heart is fully open to You!

The Journey

We engage ourselves in all kinds of journeys. Looking back over the years, there have been beautiful, exciting, and rewarding journeys that have enhanced our lives with a wide spectrum of adventure. However, there comes that time in our life when <u>*the journey*</u> will be our last, with much concern, anxiety, and challenge. How will we prepare and approach <u>*the journey*</u>?

Jesus said, *"Peace I leave with you, my peace I give unto you: not as the world giveth, give I unto you. Let not your heart be troubled, neither let it be afraid"* (John 14:27). This is a peace that only comes from God Himself. My most important journey has arrived. I am facing a life-ending disease that has no cure ... *cancer.*

Years ago, when my doctor told me I had *prostate cancer*, God gave me <u>*His Peace*</u> as I faced that alarming journey. I was led to His assurance and comfort in Psalm 94:17-19: **"Unless the Lord had given me help,** *I would soon have dwelt in the silence of death. When I said, 'My foot is slipping,' your love, O Lord, supported me. When anxiety was great within me, your consolation brought joy to my soul."* **He was my strength, my hope, and my sufficiency!**

Now, I face again the alarming words, *"You have cancer of the liver."* This is when the *"rubber hits the road,"* and the reality of my faith stands starkly before me. Do I let the boulders of doubt and unbelief overwhelm me and become the hindrance of His Peace? ... or shall His well of joy, comfort and assurance fill my life? God said, *"I took you from the ends of the earth, from the farthest corners I called you. I said,* **'You are my servant'; I have chosen you and not rejected you. So** *do not fear, for I am with you; do not be dismayed, for I am your God. I will strengthen you and help you; I will uphold you with my righteous right hand"* (Isa. 41:9-10). The challenge to me was, *"Do I really believe these words from God or do I wander in the wilderness of doubt and unbelief?"* For me, the choice was made years ago: **HE is my God, the Lord of my life, and I place unwavering faith in Him and His will ... I am His!**

The journey has started, and soon I will be given a Microwave Ablation, which isolates the tumors and eradicates the cancer by burning them with microwaves at 400 degrees. He has promised to go before me, make the crooked ways straight, and order my way. *There is no better place to be than in the Hands of God!* Am I worried, anxious, discouraged, defeated? ... **No.** My times are in His providential care. Ecstatic delight comes, for He knows the boundaries of my bewilderment and the weakness of my human nature. ***I am going to trust Him fully and see how He manifests His grace and mercy.***

The *"potholes"* that we encounter in life are but **opportunities to trust Him in and through them** ... to see the might of His power manifested *"above all we can ask or even think, through His life being lived through us"* (Eph. 3:20). Nothing comes into our life except they first pass through His permissive will. That's what Paul meant when he wrote, *"We are assured and know that all things work together and are (fitting into a plan) for good to those who love God and are the called according to (His) design and purpose"* (Rom. 8:28)(Amp.Ver.).

Therefore, I rejoice in His doing, His working, His plan, and His purpose for my life. This is but another *"step in His direction"* to see *"His mercy that is new every morning, Great is thy faithfulness"* (Lam. 3:20). **The Journey is in His plan. I shall trust Him unreservedly with all my heart.**

"According To ..."

(Eph. 3:20)

We often lose out on the impact of many precious jewels in God's Word that unveil refreshing truth from the waters that never run dry. <u>But</u> is such a word. Everything written after it supersedes all that is written before. This is so evident when Paul writes in Eph. 2, *"And you hath he quickened who were dead in trespasses and sin; wherein in times past you walked according to the course of this world, according to the prince of the power of the air, the spirit that now works in the children of disobedience: among whom also we all had our conversation in times past in the lusts of the flesh, fulfilling the desires of the flesh and of the mind; and were by nature the children of wrath even as others."* Then comes the exciting defining words, **"But God!"** What follows reveal what God does when we receive Him as Lord and Savior!

This is the <u>hinge</u> that opens the door to all God wants to do in and through us. What an awesome revelation these two words reveal, but we sometimes pass over them without realizing their eternal significance and transforming affect.

Such are the two words *"according to"* found in Eph. 3:20: *"Now unto him who is able to do immeasurably more than all we ask or imagine,* **according to** *His power that is at work within us."* These two words, *"according to,"* point us to the *infinite riches of His grace*. God provides to us His inexhaustible resources. Our faith in His covenant enables us to do the immeasurable, the superabundant, the works of His grace that is beyond our human resources and ability. When these words grip our heart, ***faith becomes a living reality,*** not hopeful desires. We draw upon *"HIS power that is at work within us."* HE becomes our **strength**, our **refuge**, our **hiding place**, our **deliverer**, and our **Mighty God!**

These are *"golden nuggets"* upon which God initiates life-changing works of grace that tremendously affect our daily walk and attitude for His glory. O to realize that we can live ***"according to** His power that is at work within us!"* It releases us from the <u>toil of striving</u> to be more than a conqueror, of <u>relying upon</u> our resources, rather than His. To lean upon <u>our</u> efforts will result in *"hay, wood, and stubble."* **To find in Christ, our sufficiency for every need,** is to live triumphantly as He lives His life through us. We are blessed with the *"jewels of His grace, the power of His might, and the comfort of His Presence."*

Oh that we might develop the practice of *"spiritual discipline"* in every phase of our life and see God in every step of our journey: claim the hidden riches found in secret places and make them stepping-stones to a triumphant faith that dares to believe and trust Him completely. It will be a transforming experience.

May we never let our attitude be that the <u>*insignificant happenings in our lives*</u> are anything less than God's Hand weaving in the small details of His design. How exciting to see the unexpected realities of His Hand of grace. When we see God in the simple things of life, we will discover *His creative and intriguing designs everywhere.*

To walk in obedience to His Word is to discipline our mind, emotions, heart, and the whole of our life to His Providential Care. Then, it is only natural that we, "b*ring into captivity every thought to the obedience of Christ"* (2 Cor. 10:5).

Meditate on the significant words in Scripture that unfold a wealth of truth ... the *"But God"* and the *"according to"* ... which will bring us into an intimate relationship with Jesus Christ and embrace, in a measure, the Majesty of God!

He Was There All The Time

I am sure there have been times in our lives when we have said, *"Where is God when I need Him most?"* We experience disturbing doubt, weakness of faith, and feel we have been left alone in this battle of devastation we now face. But, that is when the challenge of the reality of our faith comes to the forefront and says, *"Do you really believe my covenant with you and my promises to you?"*

What an alarming reality we face as we realize we are relying on <u>our</u> strength rather than His, <u>our</u> resources rather than His abundant words to us, *"Never will I leave you, never will I forsake you"* (Heb. 13:5). His Presence is made very precious when we claim, by faith, these anchors found deep in the heart of God! They stabilize our way, give unto us His strength, and fix our eyes, not on the circumstances, whatever they may be, but *on the Omnipotent One* who faithfully has already gone through what we now face. He conquered it all at Calvary! **He was there all the time!**

Can we find any more blessed word from our Savior than from those in Isaiah 43: 1-3: *"But now, this is what the Lord says ... He who created you ... He who formed you, O Israel: 'Fear not,* **for I have redeemed you; I have summoned you by name; you are mine.** *When you pass through the waters,* **I will be with you;** *when you pass through the rivers,* **they shall not sweep over you.** *When you walk through the fire,* **you will not be burned;** *the flames will not set you ablaze.* **For I am the Lord, your God, the Holy One of Israel, your Savior.'"*

When we were fearful, overcome, distressed, and feeling all alone ... we wondered where He was when we needed Him most. He was standing faithfully by our side, ready to be our sufficiency for the needs that were defeating us.

He was right where we left Him in our haste, in our concerns, in our self-independence. Then, in simple childlike faith, we took His loving Hand that lifted us up from our despair and defeat. He refreshed us with His compassion and care. He comforted and encouraged us ... then bid us to *"cast the whole of our care (all our anxieties, all our worries, all our concerns, once and for all) on Him; for He cares for us affectionately, and cares for us watchfully"* (1 Peter 5:7) (Amp.Ver.). **He was there all the time.**

We are so easily frustrated when our eyes are filled with the *devastation of the present* that overwhelms us with all of its distress. *Is He not with us **now*** as when He delivered us from the agony of disappointment and failure of our friends. Read these blessed words of encouragement: *"And I will bring the blind by a way they knew not; I will lead them in paths that they have not known: I will make darkness light before them, and crooked things straight. These things will I do unto them, and not forsake them"* (Isa. 42:16). **He was there all the time!**

How rewarding it is to transform **present destructive anxiety into constructive meaningful thoughtfulness** by exercising unreserved faith in Him, His covenants, and His promises and the leading of the Holy Spirit. Our overcoming strength is found in Christ ... our focus fixed on Christ ... and our hope secured in Christ and His faithfulness! He undergirds our life with His mercy, love and grace. *A victorious spiritual life finds reality by a life* **surrendered to God**... *a life* **controlled by God** ... *and a life* **lived for God**.

> *"Nothing is so blessed as when our outward efforts cease and our attitude becomes unforced ... when our words, prayers and our very lives become spontaneous and sincere expressions of the Life of Christ within"* (Watchman Nee).

Embers

How somber are the moments when we gaze into the burning logs of an open fireplace and recall the tales embedded in these glowing embers. Our thoughts wander through the years, reflecting on cherished memories. Our past becomes a revelation in those *burning embers,* only to be revealed as we reflect on those *precious moments that were the building blocks of our future.*

Moments: the meaningful times in our early childhood when we stretched our faith to grasp the unknown ... to reach out beyond ourselves to claim what wasn't there ... only to fall back upon the laughter and joy of the moment. The illusions of the world only enlarged our dreams of the future. As a child, we lived in a fantasy world with all of its charm and appeal: the *embers of childhood.*

The teenage years brought delight and discovery, where we explored the wonders of new experiences, the excitement of unknown ventures, embracing friends and family in significant ways that enhanced our lives. We cherish the memories of those times as we reflect on the victories and the defeats, the delight and exhilaration, the shattered and broken dreams. It was a building time as we sought to grow and mature through the stumbles on our journey. O how the embers of those glowing logs highlight these meaningful experiences and impress upon our heart how influential they were: the *embers of teens.*

How blessed also are the embers that help recall those endearing moments of family and friends. Often forgotten through the many years that have passed, we see them in the logs that turn, and new embers of silence suddenly burst with cherished thought, moments of embrace, words that touched our heart, and moments left etched upon our heart: the *embers of family and friends.*

It seems like altogether new experiences as we unfold chapter after chapter of what these embers of truth reveal each time we look into their revelations of our past. They hold such warm, meaningful, and precious times ... lest we forget. Let us ponder the depths of these embers that hold such fond and heart-searching memories: the *embers of time.*

Let us look deeper into the glowing embers as we recall the *embers of God's mercy* in withholding His judgment which we so rightly deserved. We pursued experiences in places angels fear to tread. Foolishly we sought to fulfill our way rather than His. The embers glow in their revelation of how merciful the Lord was in withholding His mercy *only to manifest His grace.* We bow in thanksgiving again and again, knowing *"had it not been for the Lord,"* where would we be today? The *embers of His mercy.*

The *embers of His infinite grace* brightly shine as they bring to our hearts how He has given unto us what we do not deserve. Interceding in times of great need and encounters that were thrust upon us, His grace was greater than all our sin. He reached down to where we were and wrapped His loving arms around us to protect, comfort and warm our hearts with His abounding grace. We reflect with cherished loving memories what these *embers of grace* reveal unto us.

Let us heed David's challenge, *"Be still and know that I am God,"* as we behold, in a measure, the infinite Love of God in all of His Majesty. *Beholding Him* brings us anew and afresh to *bow in awe of All He Is and has done for us: Embers of God that shall never perish.*

Walking In The Shadows

I have walked many times in the refreshing shadows of massive oak trees whose limbs form a canopy over a lonely country dirt road. Invigorating are the cool breezes that make their way through these trees that are hundreds of years old. More than a shield from the hot rays of the summer sun, the trees provide a peaceful refuge.

To stand in the shadow of beautiful fir trees and gaze on the enticing Blue Ridge Mountains is a most rewarding time. It is a time of reflection that stimulates our mental, emotional, and spiritual being. How needful it is for us to enjoy these meaningful times as we bask in the awesome beauty and creation of God.

I think this is what David meant when he wrote, *"He who **dwells in the secret place of the Most High** shall remain stable and fixed under the shadow of the Almighty (Whose power no foe can withstand)"* (Ps.91:1). Wow! What a blessed place He has for each of us ... but *this is only true when we appropriate what He has purchased for us and provided to us.* It is for the one who **"dwells in the secret place of the most high."** He enables us to walk in His daily companionship, compassion, and care and rejoice in the strength and joy of His presence.

Many know not such intimate relationship and are in the bondage of dwelling *in the shadow of anger, bitterness, and an unforgiving spirit.* They have subjected themselves to the penetrating ways of Satan and abide under His control and influence. They are captive of resentment and respond through their natural uncontrolled nature.

Walking under *the shadow of Bitterness* is the fruit of anger when it finds its place in self-indignation. Our ego, pride, and self-interest have been attacked, and we respond with defensive self-independence and try to shield our sinful actions and attitude. It destroys an introspective evaluation of how wretched is its influence, and how its detrimental involvement has consumed our whole personality. Only God's grace can set us free from its invasion and bring the transformation we so desperately need.

All of this entangles us when we walk under *the shadow of an unforgiving spirit* that wards off any effort to be reconciled to those we have hurt. It builds walls of a self-righteous spirit that refuses to open our hearts to the truth and to the Holy Spirit that wants to forgive and cleanse our heart. God will not condone such an attitude or use us for his glory until these ungodly attitudes and actions are confessed before His Throne of Grace. Unknowingly, we have <u>chosen</u> this course of action while beguiled by Satan. *But there is hope!*

O the Joy of Being Unshackled, Set Free, Experiencing the Might of His Power and the flow of His Love in and through us! This is ours through His mercy and grace! Can there be a greater joy than knowing the Peace of God, united in an Oneness of the Spirit, and having Him be the Lord and Authority of our life: to do away with our self-independence, pride, ego and self-righteousness?

Welcome to the loving arms of Christ, our Savior, and all the ways He wants to manifest His Life through us! He wants to adorn our life with His Life, empower our life with His power, and enable us to be *"more than conquerors through Him that loved us"* (Rom. 8:37). *The choice is ours.* **"He who dwells in the secret place of the Most High shall remain stable and fixed under the shadow of the Almighty"** (Ps. 91:1).

"He Wholly Followed The Lord"

(Joshua 14:14)

I have often thought, "What does it mean for me to wholly follow the Lord?" There must be a radical difference between one who follows Him in any other way than *wholly*. I've seen many who have been faithful in following the creeds, traditions, and customs of the Church. Many say, "O I have faith to wholly follow the Lord." Unfortunately, it is a vacillating faith, one of compromise, following afar off as Peter. They are sincere but they have *missed the mark* when their life does not coincide with the demands of discipleship that GOD sets forth in His Word. God said, **"If any man will follow me, let him deny himself and take up his cross daily and follow me"** (Luke 9:23).

We cannot determine what's right unless we are directed by the Holy Spirit Who will reveal what it means *"to follow Him wholly."* From the passage in Joshua, as the 12 spies reported back to Moses, it meant they would either believe God ... or determine within their own carnal nature what was best for them. There was no middle ground, no place for compromise. Without hesitation, they would dare to trust HIM wholly ... or be governed by their own ungodly desires. They stood at the crossroads of a decision that would govern the whole of their life.

What a faithful declaration, unrelenting confidence, and unwavering trust by Caleb and Joshua in the Omnipotent One. There was no question as to their decision: *"We are well able to overcome."* Why? Because their faith was without reservation in God! Their faith was inscribed on their hearts long ago. Its reality comes forth when it is put to the test. True faith is for all of our life for all occasions.

But look a little further and notice the urgency of his decision: *"Let us go up **at once** and possess it."* There was no hesitancy, debate, or any other consideration. True faith brooks no delay but acts upon His leading ... *Now.* Why do we have such a difficult time following the Lord? Because we have a divided heart, we are not wholly committed, and our faith often follows the life-style we desire. *We sacrifice "God's Best" for a shallow pretense and compromised faith.*

O, to follow Him fully! Fully? Yes, fully. No strings attached, without reservation, completely His in every phase of our life ... *fully!* To surrender our will to His and make Him the Lord and Authority of our life is to know *His Peace* that passes understanding, *His Mercy* that endures forever, *His Grace* that knows no bounds, and *His infinite Love* that is beyond our understanding! Are you willing to sacrifice all of this to follow y*our way and will*?

The Lord wants to fill us with His Love and live His Life through us, and be endowed with His virtues. This can only be a reality when we *"follow Him fully!"* To plunder in the way of our selfish will is sure defeat. To surrender our will to His Lordship is *awesome victory.* Our life becomes eternally effective when the fullness and adequacy of Christ engulfs our life and is our authoritative power. God desires to put His truth into the minds of His disciples ... His Compassion in their hearts ... His Will into their lives ... and make His Lordship Sovereign.

*Where there is **unerring wisdom** to direct our way, **almighty power** to execute His plan, a **receptive and responsive spirit by us to follow Him wholly** ... no difficulty can exist which cannot be overruled by His Power:* **"He wholly followed the Lord"** (Joshua 14:14).

"Rejoice In The Lord Always"

(Phil. 4:4)

True rejoicing in the Lord often comes during or after a devastating trial or persecution. We find this throughout Scripture and among the new converts that Paul had led to believing faith in Christ. Paul and Barnabas left these new converts at Antioch and Pisidia because of the severe persecution. Did these new Believers complain and plead with the Apostles to stay and care for their spiritual welfare? No. It was an opportunity for others to hear the Gospel from Paul and Barnabas. They also were confident the Holy Spirit that dwelt within them would provide for their every need.

The Scripture reads, *"And the disciples were filled with great joy and with the Holy Ghost."* Why? These Believers exercised great faith in trusting God amidst severe persecution even though they were babes in Christ. It is not whether we have *faith* but rather *in WHOM our faith is fixed*. Persecution, adversities, and hostile opposition abound wherever the stakes of the Gospel are implanted.

We often wonder why God permits the trials and adversities of life. We often become frustrated, impatient, and weary when we encounter these experiences. In yielding to His authority and control when they befall us, they become determining factors to develop in us a depth of His grace, love, and mercy we have never known before. For it is *in* the trial, *in* the adversity, *in* our difficulty, and *in* the darkness of these hours, that the light of His Presence and Power shines brightest. *"I have learned to love the darkness of sorrow; there you can see the brightness of His face"* Madame Guyon.

Faith lifts us <u>above</u> our circumstances while we are yet <u>in them</u>. It gives sustenance to the Believer and provides evidence of the truth and reality that will secure us from falling whatever the trial may be. When we exercise true faith, claiming a promise God has given to us, we are putting our confidence, trust and reliance in the *"infallible character of God and the merits of His Son Jesus Christ!"*

It is *'insignificant'* where we are ... but *'very significant'* in whom we trust where we are. People today are looking for faith in God that is real, a faith that finds its way into our life and makes a transforming change in the way we live *in the times of trial.* True faith in Christ results in the virtues of Christ being lived through us by His Indwelling Presence and Power.

"This is the **<u>Exchanged Life</u>**. *The secret is simple, yet it is profound. It is an obtainment, not an attainment. It is a gift received, not an achievement to be earned. It is from above, not from within us. It is a life that arises out of death to ourselves, not from any <u>deeds we have done</u>.* (Dr. V. Raymond Edman) God gives us His joy whereby we sing with the new Believers under severe tribulation, **"Rejoice in the Lord always; and again I say rejoice"** (Phil. 4:4).

Let us thank Him for all the way *"He has led us"* and trust Him for all the way *"that is yet before us."* From all we have received <u>hitherto</u>, let us claim, by faith, all that is <u>henceforth</u>. Those who joyfully leave everything in God's Hand will eventually see God's Hand in everything!

What is the challenge before us today? *"Enlarge your place, stretch your tent, do not hold back, lengthen the cords and strengthen the stakes"* (Isa. 54:2).

These are stepping-stones that, when joined with unwavering faith in Christ, will carry us to *knowing the unspeakable Joy of the Lord!* Dare to believe, trust Him fully, and walk in His triumphant companionship daily: **"Rejoice in the Lord always; again I say rejoice."**

Hearken Unto Me

As a whole, we are a stubborn, ungrateful people. In our distress, we fervently call on God to deliver us from the devastating circumstance we are in. We recognize our dilemma and the trying conditions for which we often conclude that there is no way out. Fervent prayer and intercession is made, and then ... GOD, in His mercy and grace, brings deliverance! ... *"This poor man cried, and the Lord heard him, and saved him out of all his troubles"* (Ps. 34:6).

On their solemn feast day, Israel pulled out all the stops as they sang aloud unto God ... made a joyful noise unto the God of Jacob ... and with many instruments and in jubilant song and praise, rejoiced in all God had done for them (Ps. 81: 1-3). It was a time of great celebration, an occasion in which they stood in awe of the greatness of God

Then God said, *"I removed thy shoulder from the burden: thy hands were delivered from the pots. Thou callest in trouble, and I delivered thee; I answered thee in the secret place of thunder: I proved thee at the waters of Meribah"* (vs. 6-7). God gave them a simple command to follow: **"hearken unto Me ... open thy mouth and I will fill it."**

You might have assumed they would have said, "What an incredible, gracious God we have. Let us follow and worship Him alone that He may lead, protect, deliver, and bless us as He has promised." **But then we read the sad commentary of their hearts:** *"But my people would not hearken to my voice: and Israel would have none of me. So I gave them up: and they walked in their own counsels"* (vs. 11-12). They were stubborn, ungrateful, self-centered and independent, with ungodly determination to fulfill their selfish lust. ***That's inconceivable ... yet, as they did, so we do***.

This is a concise image of us when we choose to follow <u>our ways</u> rather than Christ being the priority and authority of our life. *"I removed thy shoulder from the burden ... thy hands were delivered from the pots ... I delivered thee ... I proved thee ... open your mouth and I will fill it."* God has covenanted to do this for each of us and fill our hearts in an overflowing measure ... BUT, **as they did, so do we!**

They turned their backs on what God had done in preference to their lustful desires and God said, *"So I gave them up ... "* What a despicable appalling choice they made. Do we find ourselves responding in the same way? You might say, "Oh I wouldn't do what they did. I go to church, give liberally, and seek to follow Him as best as <u>I</u> can."

There are many ways in which we do not obey His command, *"Hearken unto Me."* We set our own standard of obedience ... march to the beat of <u>our</u> desires ... live in the lustful choices of <u>our lifestyle</u> ... and set the stage of *our performance* and follow dutifully! There is no compromise when we follow Him in every phase of our life. A.W. Tozer said this about Truth: "Truth is a glorious but hard master. It makes moral demands upon us. It claims the sovereign right to control us, to strip us, even to slay us as it chooses. Truth will never stoop to be a servant but requires that all men serve it. It never flatters men and never compromises with them. It demands all or nothing and refuses to be used or patronized. It will be all in all or it will withdraw into silence."

His truth is transparent, profound, sincere and factual, with integrity and depth of character. There is no pretense or hypocrisy. It demands high moral standards that require us to surrender our right to His control and authority. Heed His command ... **"Hearken unto Me."** ... without reservation.

Show Me ... Teach Me ... Lead Me

Have you ever wondered why we progress so slowly in our spiritual life? We seem to strive and seek to grow in grace but see so little evidence of being embraced with the fruit of the Spirit. Maybe we should follow David's path and see God fill our lives with things beyond our capabilities. In Ps. 27:4-5, David says, **"Show me** *thy ways, O Lord;* **teach me** *thy paths.* **Lead me** *in thy truth, and teach me: for thou art the God of salvation;* **on thee do I wait all the day.***"*

David was desirous to have God fill his life with all He had for him and could do through him. He realized his exalted position as King of Israel was an incredible responsibility. Within his own ability, he was incapable of being Israel's King as well as being triumphant in his own spiritual relationship with God. Therefore, he cries out to God, *"Show me ... Teach me ... Lead me ... for on Thee do I wait all the day."*

"Show me thy ways." David had a intense longing to see God in every phase of his life and to make His virtues a reality in his life. He wanted to see God manifest His mighty power in his walk. Moses was overwhelmed when he was with God on the mount and said, *"... If I have found grace in thy sight,* **show me now thy way,** *that I may know thee ... and he said, I beseech thee,* **show me thy glory"** (Ex. 33:13, 18). How blessed for God to *show unto us* the greatness of His power in doing that which surpasses our capabilities.

Joshua, Jeremiah, Job, Habakkuk, Paul, Peter, and countless others gave their lives–with some being burned at the stake–rather than recant their heart's desire to see God in the wonders of His grace. *"Show me thy ways O Lord."*

"Teach me thy paths." O for the hunger of being taught. How necessary it is to have a mentor who shows evidence in his walk that he is applying God's Truth fully to his life and is daily "walking with the Lord!" But what are the <u>paths of God</u>?

Paul's prayer for the new Believers was, *"That God, the Father of glory, may give you the Spirit of wisdom and revelation in the knowledge of Himself"* (Eph. 1: 17). Without that Spirit, especially sought and received, and yielded to in great traceableness, the truths of His Word will remain a hidden mystery. With that teaching, we shall be *"filled with the knowledge of God's Will in all wisdom and spiritual understanding."* We shall learn to know what passeth knowledge and be brought to experience that His power is able to impact our lives with only what He can do. *"O the depth of the riches both of the wisdom and knowledge of God. How unsearchable are His judgments, and His ways past finding out"* (Rom. 11:33). *"Teach me thy paths."*

"Lead me in Thy truth ... on Thee do I wait all the day." Do you notice Whom he is depending upon to bring all of this about? *No one less than God Himself.* "The aim of our life must ever be to make God's standard the object of our unceasing desire. God's Spirit has been given us to reveal Christ and His life to us. No true progress can be made until with purpose of heart we consent in everything we shall live in immediate and unceasing dependence on the power of the Holy Spirit" (Andrew Murray).

The one great object of God, in the gift of the Holy Spirit, was to fit His people for being and doing what they cannot be or do within themselves. May we start with these three challenges: *Show me ... Teach me ... Lead me.*

Love That Knows No Bounds

We often speak of love, dedication sacrifice, and commitment, but seldom see it manifested in a moving life-changing way. These Godly qualities should characterize the life of every Believer. This is the true account of the renowned artist, Albrecht Durer.

"Back in the fifteenth century, in a tiny village near Nuremberg, lived a family with eighteen children. In order merely to keep food on the table for this mob, the father and head of the household, a goldsmith by profession, worked almost eighteen hours a day at his trade and any other paying chore he could find in the neighborhood.

Two of the sons, Albrecht and Albert, had a dream. They both wanted to pursue their talent for art, but they knew full well that their father would never be financially able to send either of them to Nuremberg to study at the Academy. After many long discussions at night in their crowded bed, the two boys finally worked out a pact. They would toss a coin. The loser would go down into the nearby mines and, with his earnings, support his brother while he attended the Academy. Then, when that brother who won the toss completed his studies, in four years, he would support the other brother at the Academy. They tossed a coin and Albrecht Durer won the toss and went off to Nuremberg.

Albert went down into the dangerous mines and, for the next four years, financed his brother, whose work at the Academy was almost an immediate sensation. Albrecht's etchings, his woodcuts, and his oils were far better than those of most of his professors, and by the time he graduated, he was beginning to earn considerable fees for his commissioned works.

When the young artist returned to his village, the Durer family held a festive dinner on their lawn to celebrate Albrecht's triumphant homecoming. After a long and memorable meal, punctuated with music and laughter, Albrecht rose from his honored position at the head of the table to drink a toast to his beloved brother for the years of sacrifice that had enabled Albrecht to fulfill his ambition. His closing words were, "And now, Albert, blessed brother of mine, now it is your turn. Now you can go to Nuremberg to pursue your dream, and I will take care of you."

All heads turned in eager expectation to the far end of the table where Albert sat, tears streaming down his pale face, shaking his lowered head from side to side while he sobbed and repeated, over and over, "No ...no....no ...no."

Finally, Albert rose and wiped the tears from his cheeks. He glanced down the long table at the faces he loved, and then, holding his hands close to his right cheek, he said softly, "No, brother. I cannot go to Nuremberg. It is too late for me. Look ... Look what four years in the mines have done to my hands! The bones in every finger have been smashed at least once, and lately I have been suffering from arthritis so badly in my right hand that I cannot even hold a glass to return your toast, much less make delicate lines on parchment or canvas with a pen or a brush. No, brother ...for me it is too late."

Albrecht Durer's hundreds of masterful portraits, pen and silver-point sketches, water colors, charcoals, woodcrafts, and copper engravings hang in every great museum in the world. His tribute of love to his brother ... "The Praying Hands" (Author Unknown).

What an incredible touching account of love, sacrifice and devotion given to be a blessing and encouragement to another. Lord, help us that such virtues are manifested in our life for your glory!

God Is My Portion

The framework of our choices have made us *'who we are.'* How tremendous is the transformation of one who once delighted in the deceitful delusions of the world and who now renounces it as sincerely as he ever loved it. Grace has made him a *"new creation in Christ; the old has gone, the new has come"* 2 Cor. 5:17, NIV. The Believer's delight is now God, as exceedingly great and glorious. God is the one object of his choice and his eternal portion.

To the Believer there is nothing in this world that can compete or match up to the incomparable Christ. He concludes that the riches, worldly pleasures and honors are lighter than vanity. Because of the Atonement Christ, he is utterly crucified to them all. *"God forbid that I should glory, save in the cross of our Lord Jesus Christ, by who the world is crucified unto me, and I unto the world"* Gal. 46:14.

David desired nothing greater than the divine presence of God. *"One thing have I desired of the Lord, that I will seek after; that I may dwell in the house of the Lord all the days of my life, to behold the beauty of the Lord, and to inquire in his temple"* Ps. 27:4. **God was his portion!**

Paul had as much of this world's grandeur and honor as any man who ever lived. When he met God, his life was transformed. *"But what things were gain to me, those I counted loss for Christ. Yea, doubtless, and I count all things but loss for the Excellency of Christ Jesus my Lord: for I have suffered the loss of all things, and do count them as dung, that I may win Christ"* Phil. 3:7-8. **God was his portion!**

Such a choice is not peculiar to these distinguished servants of God. Down through the ages there have been the martyrs of the faith, many burned at the stake, missionaries who sacrificed their life in unknown regions, and countless others who stood true to God rather than recant their faith and commitment to God. **God was their portion!**

He is our ever-present portion. God is everywhere to be our ever-present help. I found Him ever so present in foxholes in W.W.II. *"Whither shall I go from thy Spirit? Or whither shall I flee from thy presence? If I ascend up into heaven, thou art there: if I make my bed in hell, behold thou art there. If I take the wings of the morning, and dwell in the uttermost parts of the sea; even there shall thy hand lead me, and thy right hand shall hold me" Ps. 139: 7-10.*

He is our all-sufficient portion. What can avail the unbeliever when enduring excruciating pains? What relief can afford him under the agonies of a guilty conscience? What can appease him from the fears of death? In the absence of all temporal comforts, the Believer can take courage and rejoice in knowing, *"The Lord is my shepherd; I shall not want ... Though I walk through the shadow of death, I will fear no evil: for thou art with me; thy rod and thy staff they comfort me" Ps. 23:1,4.* **He is their portion!**

He is my eternal portion. All of life's temporal things we will part with at last. We will carry nothing with us into eternity. But, if *"God is our portion"* we shall possess Him forever in all His glory. *"For now we see through a glass, darkly; but then face to face: now I know in part; but then shall I know even as also I am known" 1 Cor. 13:12.*

*"***Now** *we taste of the streams;* **then** *shall we drink at the fountainhead.* **Now** *our capacity to enjoy Him is but small;* **then** *all our faculties will be wonderfully enlarged.* **Now** *our delight in Him is transient;* **then***, without intermission or end" Charles Simeon.* **GOD IS MY PORTION!**

The Choice Is Ours

How little there is of true faith in God in the world! It seems everyone has there own *"standard to live by"* which they consider will be approved by God on the Day of Judgment. If being called after the name of Christ were sufficient, there would be a large flock of His follows. If to faithfully attend worship services, adhere to His ordinances, and 'profess' faith in God were enough, there would be many in the way to heaven. But *God has His Standard of Reconciliation* He plainly gave in His Word. *He is to be our Savior, Lord, and Sovereign Authority!* He will judge us, *not according to our professions,* **but according to our practice ... the manifestation of a faith that is real and effectually supplied in every phase of our life.**

God can never be *our portion* unless we deliberately choose Him in preference to all others. Does the passion of our devotion and commitment to God confirm the strength of our desires after God? How does our zeal for God compare to those who follow enthusiastically and fervently the worldly things of time and sense? The world longs to see faith that is real and demonstrates their commitment to God in all of their life. It is not just a simple 'profession' but our faith in His Atonement on Calvary and the ***possession of the Living Christ and His possession of all of us.***

Being a living example of the in-living Christ is a *'becoming process.'* The Holy Spirit does not have full control of our life until we deliberately surrender our will to His Authority and control. We take on a "new creative nature born of God and manifested to others by the power of the Holy Spirit. As Paul so emphatically wrote, *"I am crucified with Christ: nevertheless I live; yet not I, but Christ liveth in me: and the life which I now live in the flesh I live by the faith of the Son of God, who loved me, and gave himself for me' Gal. 2:20.*

Keith Hunt, who was the Regional Director of Inter-Varsity Christian Fellowship, was having a meeting with a group of international students from the University. At the close of the meeting one of the foreign students expressed his appreciation for his hospitality. He said, "I am impressed with the Christian students, they have something I don't have. I'm interested in Christianity. What does it take to be a Christian?"

Keith said, "First, you must give your life to Jesus Christ without reservation and receive Him as your personal Savior. Give you life totally and completely unto Christ." The young student replied, "O I couldn't do that. It would cost me my political standing, I would be ostracized by my family, my friends would turn from me, I could even be killed." Keith said, "Well if you ever decide to surrender your heart to the Lord, I would love to hear from you."

The next morning about 6:15 the doorbell rang, and who should be there but this foreign student. He said, "Mr. Hunt I have been up all night thinking thorough what you said. *If that what it takes, I'm ready to pay the price.*" Keith opened the Scriptures to him and led him to faith in Christ.

Really, that's what it's all about! There comes a time and place in all of our lives where we must make a break, when we cut loose of our life and give it totally and unconditionally to Christ as our Savior and Lord. Jesus said, *"If any man will come after me, let him deny himself and take up his cross daily, and follow me. For whosoever will save his life shall lose it: but whosoever will lose his life for my sake, the same shall find it. For what is a man advantaged, if he gain the whole world, and lose himself, or be a castaway?" Luke 9:23-25.* **The choice is yours.**

How Then Shall We Live?

One of the great concerns among evangelical leaders is the attitude that prevails with the average Christian. Many think that having found Christ as their Savior, *they no longer need to seek Him.* They believe that attending the customs and traditions of the Church is sufficient for their faith, therefore there's no need to read and study the Bible, pray, witness, and seek fellowship with other Believers.

These things are necessary if we are to 'grow in grace and mature as a Believer.' Receiving Jesus Christ as our Savior is the *"beginning"* of our walk with the Lord. We need to nurture, encourage, and seek to follow the Lord *now* in every phase of our life as we surrender to His Lordship and Providential Authority of our life.

A few years ago, the late Charles Colson, the former confident and White House hatchet man, wrote a challenging book entitled, *"How Then Shall We Live."* The premise of his book was the 'costly grace' that provided our salvation through Jesus Christ and our accountability living in response to His love. It is a penetrating and invasive book to the passive life-style of the average Believer.

During a visit to Australia, a well-known radio host interviewed Charles Colson. As the interview drew to a close, he posed one last question. "Mr. Colson, you are an unusual person. You have achieved the pinnacle of secular success. The goals most men strive their whole life for, you have accomplished. However, you have seen it all collapse as you fell from the 'inner circle' of the White House to a Federal Prison, after the Watergate investigation. It is like having lived two lives. How do you sum up the meaning of those two lives?

Charles Colson glanced at the clock and realized he had only 20 seconds left in the live broadcast. Then in a flash the short answer came. *"If my life stands for anything, it is the Truth and Teaching of Jesus Christ." "Whosoever wants to save his life will lose it. But whosoever loses his life for my sake and the Gospel's, will find it. What good will it be for a man if he gains the whole world, yet forfeits his own soul?" Matt. 16:25-26.*

With those profound words we went off the air. Certainly those words embody a staggering paradox. *"I spent the first forty years of my life seeking the whole world to the neglect of my soul. What I couldn't find in my quest for power and success, true security and meaning, I discovered in a Federal Prison where all worldly props were stripped away from me. I lost my life that I might find 'true life' in Jesus Christ!"*

The essence of sin is ... "my claim to my right to myself." I do not want to surrender my right to control my life. I want to make my decisions and live as 'the captain of my fate!' God never forces a man to surrender to His will to Him. He waits until he *'yields up'* his will without reservation to God. He writes over his life, *"He is Mine"* Isaiah 43:1-3. **What do we lose? ... Our Life. What do we gain? ... HIS LIFE!**

People everywhere are expending their time, energy, and abilities to *'gain'* what they cannot keep, *'buy'* what they do not need and *'accumulate'* money they will never spend.

Jim Elliott, a martyred missionary in Ecuador wrote ... **"He Is No Fool Who Gives What He Cannot Keep To Gain What He Cannot Lose."**

The Surety Of Our Faith

"I know O Lord, that a man's life is not his own; it is not in man to direct his steps" Jer. 10:23. One of the greatest blessings in our spiritual journey is the realization that *'we'* are weak, feeble and vulnerable in our abilities and resources ... but *in Christ*, we have access to His wisdom, strength, power and sufficiency. As we dare to trust Him, He has promised to direct our steps and order our way (Prov. 3:5-6).

Nothing comes into the life of a Believer except it first goes through the heart and will of God. When we come to the crossroads of a devastating experience, we have the free will to choose the direction we take. We are challenged to trust Him. Therefore, *we should accept what He has allowed, trust Him for what we don't understand, and cast our care without reservation on Him (I Peter 5:7).*

God watches over those who dare to trust Him. **He restrains our adversaries (Ps. 4:6,7). He comforts and assures us** *of His presence and power (Isa. 43:1-3).* **He imparts to us** *temporal and spiritual blessings (Matt. 6:33).* **He hears and answers** *our supplications (John 15:7 and Jer. 33:3).* **He communes with us** *as sons and daughters (2 Cor. 6:18).* **He takes upon Himself** *the management of our concerns (Isa. 46:4). How blessed to dare to believe and trust Him fully!*

We say He is **Omnipotent** (All powerful), yet we fail so miserably to trust Him in the encounters we face. We say He is **Omniscient** (Knows everything infinitely), yet we live as if we are in complete control of our life and do not need Him to direct our way or restrain us from selfish indiscretion. We read that He is **Omnipres-**

ent (Present everywhere at all times). Yet we live within the boundaries of our finite restrictions. *Without holiness* no man will see the Lord. However, we exert little if any effort to make holiness our chief concern and priority of our life.

"It is one thing to know intellectually the wonderful doctrines of His grace, but quite another to see them experimentally active in our spiritual walk. It is one thing to believe the Scriptures to be inerrant and divinely inspired, but another to live in awe of their Divine Authority and Sovereign rule of our life. It is one thing to be convinced that Jesus Christ is the Son of God, the King of kings, but yet another to surrender to His Lordship and live in personal subjection to Him in every phase of our life" ... Arthur Pink.

I know my own sinfulness and failures, but I also know the virtue of His cleansing blood. I know well my own weakness and vulnerability, but I also know the Sufficiency of His Grace. I know the deceitfulness and treachery of my heart, but I also know the surety of His mercy. I know well the faulty ways of my walk, but I also know the *"exceeding great and precious promises, that by these you might be partakers of the divine nature"* 2 Peter 1:4.

With renewed purpose of heart, we should live each day to the maximum for His glory ... seize every opportunity God places in our path ... seek to encourage and strengthen others ... and be a blessing to everyone we meet. We should align our lives with the current of God's love and will.

May His Word be the foundation of our confidence, the surety of our consolation and sufficiency for our every need. May the Lord empower us, manifest His love in us, and live His life through us in an abounding measure ... that others may see Christ only. Amen.

I Remember

(Message given by Edward Powell on Memorial Day Service 2014, at the Tomoka Christian Church in Ormond Beach, Florida)

In our age of selfish interest and unconcern, we find very few whose lives **"remember in any significant way"** *the life-changing encounters that have affected the lives of millions.* They are vivid *in the minds of those who took part and those whose lives were ingrained by the tragedies that occurred. Let me mention a few that changed my life forever.*

I REMEMBER ... **December 7, 1941** ... **Pearl Harbor** ... **the surprise attack** by the Japanese that left 2402 dead and 1282 military personnel wounded. Our Pacific Fleet and Air Force were severely shattered. That began our War with Japan that took an immeasurable toll in the lives of heroic fighting men who fought in the Pacific sector.

I REMEMBER ... Iwo Jima, Guadalcanal, Midway, Wake Island, Coral Sea and others that took a staggering toll in dead and wounded troops.

I REMEMBER ... The **Bataan Death March** ... **April 9, 1942** ... in the Philippines, where 72,000 American and Philippine POW's were forced to march 80 miles through jungle and gravel roads. Over 7000 lives perished.

I REMEMBER ... **December 11, 1941** ... **Germany and Italy declared War** on the U.S., and we responded by committing our Country to a World War conflict.

*I REMEMBER … **June 6, 1944 … D-DAY… Allied Forces** landed on the beaches of Normandy and initiated our involvement in the European Theater where the blood and lives of thousands of young heroic men were given.*

I saw the devastating remains** of that awesome tragedy that took place on the beaches of Omaha and Utah … I climbed the same steep cliff those heroic men did at Omaha Beach. As I reached the top of the cliff, there were 2500 white crosses for those who lost their lives in that tragic invasion and days that followed it. **The reality of war stood forcibly before me. I stood in awe of the price of blood and life that had been sacrificed for our freedom.

*I REMEMBER … **The Holocaust … The Inhumane Barbaric Horror** of untold millions that were enslaved in the concentration camps of Germany that were beyond belief. There were nine million Jews living in Germany of which six million died or were exterminated in the Camps along with five to eleven million others from various nations. Such inhumane action surpasses our imagination.*

*I REMEMBER … **August 6th and 9th 1945 … Atom Bombs** destroyed Hiroshima and Nagasaki, which led to the surrender of Japan. This was a tragedy we trust will never happen again.*

*I REMEMBER … **Sept. 2, 1945 … Japan Unconditionally Surrendered** on the Battleship, USS Missouri, to our Supreme Allied Commander, Gen. Douglas McArthur, who vowed as he left the Philippines, "I Shall Return!" And return he did!*

*I REMEMBER … **May 7, 1945 … Germany surrendered** at Reims, France, ending the most horrendous war in history, a war that inscribed its horror with Death, Dismay and Devastation on the lives of untold Millions.*

*I REMEMBER … **September 11, 2001 … The Twin Towers attack.** We all were shocked and in disbelief that such a disaster could possibly happen … but it did! With unerring accuracy, the terrorists flew <u>our</u> aircraft directly into the Twin Tower buildings and into the Pentagon.*

Can we possibly forget the **D**eath, **H**orror, **F**ear, **C**onfusion, **D**ismay, **H**eartache, and **U**nbelievable **T**rauma *of this tragedy? Death and Disaster stood hand in hand as thousands sought to rescue and save as many as possible.*

I REMEMBER ... The many accounts of heroic compassion *and concern demonstrated by countless people during this tragedy. Firefighters, Policemen, and a vast array of public service organizations responded without hesitation.*

One account, *hidden among the rescue efforts, was the "unheralded task" of hundreds of boats of every description evacuating stranded people on the banks of the Hudson River. These boat owners were motivated by ... "I have to go and help!" Incredibly, during the course of nine hours, 500,000 people were lifted by these boats to safety, an inconceivable story I only heard eleven years afterward.*

I REMEMBER ... My daughter *and her husband were on a flight from Paris back to the U.S. when, two hours before they were due to land, word was received by their pilot that all airports in the U.S. were shut down. They landed in Nova Scotia in an airport that was not built to accommodate a Jumbo Jet that flew transcontinental flights. Miraculously, more than two-dozen of these large aircraft jammed this small airport to find safety. Only the grace of God enabled care for these thousands of passengers and made it possible for the pilots to land and later take off from this very small local airport.*

Such Horrific Events *have been indelibly inscribed on my heart in a way that has* **changed my perspective of life immeasurably.** *The history of these tragedies should awaken us to the true values of life ... as the supreme cost of countless lives stand starkly before us.*

Sir Winston Churchill, *the renowned orator and England's Prime Minister during WWII, in speaking to his Parliament on August 20, 1940 about the efforts of the RAF in the air battles over England, said, "Never in the field of human conflict* **was so much owed by so many to so few."** *So it can be said of our Servicemen as well.*

Do we have a debt to those who have given their all ... to those who bear the scars and the tragic memories of these monumental events for the rest of their lives? They gave unreservedly ... that we might be blessed with Freedom and Liberty, Peace and Hope, Friends and Loved Ones?

YES, we are forever indebted! We should show such response with deep concern for our Country and with personal moral obligation to live Responsible, Principled, and Dedicated lives ... to preserve what so many paid the ultimate price for. We should reach out to others and live beyond ourselves in His strength and power.

I REMEMBER ... when the Sergeant came into our barracks at the Port of Embarkation, Camp Shanks, N.Y., and shouted, "We're moving out in 10 minutes." We were shuttled to the docks of New York City to be shipped overseas and soon to be engaged in War.

As I walked up the gangplank, the Captain and his Staff were wishing us "God Speed" to what he knew was before us. As I approached the Captain, I asked him, "What is the name of this BOAT?" He said, "Son, this is not a Boat. This is HMS, the renowned Queen Mary ... 92,000 tons of legendary beauty." The ship was built to accommodate 3,200 passengers. It was renovated into a Troop Ship that would now take 20,000 of us to Europe.

I REMEMBER ... cruising by the Statue of Liberty, which I had never seen before. As I stood on the deck, I thought this may be the last time I will see this awesome Tribute of Freedom. I prayed, "Lord if it is your will that I should return, I'll give you all the praise and glory." It is only by His grace that I am here today."

I REMEMBER ... when we landed in Scotland, HE WAS THERE ... into England, HE WAS THERE ... Finally to France, Belgium, and Germany ... HE WAS THERE!

I REMEMBER ... 1944, being on the front line of battle, as a machine gunner with the 1st Division ... We were to go through the Hurtgen Forest to Cologne in four days.

The Battle of the Bulge was intense and those four days turned into six horrifying weeks. It was the bloodiest and most decisive battle of the war. By comparison, we have lost over 5,000 men in Afghanistan and Iraq in the last five years. In the Battle of the Bulge, we lost 55,000 men and 160,000 wounded in SIX WEEKS! The Germans lost many more.

I REMEMBER ... asking the Lord to have someone to help me when I would either be killed or wounded. I did not feel I would go on much longer without facing such a tragedy.

*It was only three days later, around 11:30 at night ... I was in a shallow foxhole, covered with snow and bitter cold. The Germans threw in a heavy artillery barrage, trying to wipe out our position. Shells were exploding everywhere. One hit very close to our foxhole, and I turned to my buddy and said, "Wow, that's the closest one yet!" Just then, a shell exploded in a tree burst above us, and the shrapnel came screaming down, critically wounding both of us. Both of my forearms and a right leg were almost blown off, and a piece of shrapnel, half the size of your thumb, pierced the back of my neck, just missing my spine a quarter of an inch ... but **HE WAS THERE!***

They pulled me out of my foxhole, dragged me to a jeep, and laid me across the hood to take me back to a first-aid tent behind the front line. I was bleeding so freely, I didn't think I would live to get there. Shells were still exploding everywhere.

Then ... God gave me a "Song in the Night," and I started singing, "Only Trust Him, He will save you, He will save you now." I was going to sing my way right into the Presence of the Lord.

Let me encourage you ... Whatever circumstances you are facing today, however devastating ... God can give you a "Song in the Night!" ... lift you out of the doldrums of Despair, Discouragement, and Defeat and be your Mighty Refuge, Strength and Deliverer.

At the first-aid tent, they gave me a shot of morphine, bandaged my arms and leg, using pieces of an orange crate for splints, and we started an 8-hour trip back to Liege, Belgium, to the Field Hospital. It was a school that had been converted into a hospital. The operating room was in the cafeteria with dozens of tables used to operate on.

I REMEMBER ... after they operated, the Doctor came in to see me and gave such a blessed word of encouragement. He said, "We're sending you back to the USA. The War is over for you. We can bind up, but only God can heal!" How blessed that was to me. How gracious is the Lord! That began two and a half years of hospitalization and many surgeries, as they rebuilt my arms and leg.

On one occasion in England, five Doctors stood by my bed to examine my right arm, which they shielded with a sheet so I couldn't see it. The Surgeon came in that night and started talking with me. I said, "Doc, are you trying to tell me that you're going to amputate my right arm?" He said, "Yes, there's not enough left that we can save it." I said, "Well if that's the best you can do, let's get on with it. When will you operate?" He said, "Seven o'clock tomorrow morning."

After he left, I had a session with the Lord and said, "Lord, you know I don't want to lose my right arm, but Thy will be done!" I learned a precious lesson that night. The way to Victory and Peace ... is Complete Resignation to His Will!

After they put me to sleep in the operating room, one of the Doctors said, "Let's take one more look at his arm and see if there's any way we can save it." They found my radial pulse was still intact and decided not to *amputate my arm. With multiple operations of a large skin graft and an extensive bone graft, they saved my arm.*

After many operations *and two and a half years in Army hospitals, I was ready to be discharged. When I was given my Discharge papers, what do you think they typed in their closing statement? "Recommended for further service!" Are you kidding me? I was like a Hardware Store ... full of nuts and bolts, screws, staples, wires and plates, and what have you. I was an Erector Set on two legs!*

I REMEMBER ... During my last few months in the hospital, *I met my future wife, Millie. God had led her to rent a room in my parent's house in Jacksonville, FL. After meeting her, I made several trips on weekends from the Army Hospital in Augusta, Georgia to Jacksonville to see her. There was a very important attraction and motivation that prompted my trips home.*

Millie and I were married *as the Lord brought our hearts together by His grace. But, I was having difficulty with civilian life. When I was in the Hospital, there was always someone worse off than me. We would make fun of one another about how bad we looked. It was a kind of therapy for us. But, when I was discharged ... I was the odd fellow on the block.*

Whenever I wore a short sleeve shirt, I noticed that people would drop their eyes and focus on my arms. I knew what they were thinking, and I was embarrassed that my arms were so twisted, scarred and disfigured. I vowed to never wear a short sleeve shirt again.

Soon it was my birthday. *What do you think Millie gave me for my birthday? Two Short Sleeve Shirts! I was devastated. I realized I had a psychological problem. That night I prayed and told the Lord of my dilemma. In His Grace, He said, "Are you embarrassed by what I did for you? Had it not been for Me, you would not have survived, much less have your arms and leg today." I asked the Lord for forgiveness for my selfish concern. God* *changed my attitude and the focus of my life. Instead of being embarrassed now ... my arms are Trophies of His Grace.*

My question for all of us this morning is ... HOW THEN SHALL WE LIVE? Shall we join the many, *who, without regard to countless tragic events, live without concern, caring only for their selfish life and living in the bondage of their self-appointed ways?*

God forbid *that we should take such a passive unconcern as so many do today! Let us focus not on our self-centered life, with all of its shallow values and superficial attractions, but on a life, which is Meaningful, Fulfilling, and Eternal ... Lived in God's strength for His honor and glory.*

May those Horrific Events of the Past be forever engraved on our hearts and create the eternal gratitude and thanksgiving they command ... They have been purchased at an immeasurable price in both killed and wounded.
I REMEMBER ... Let us never, never, never forget!

Additional copies of

"IN TIMES LIKE THESE"

Available at www.createspace/4002698,
and Amazon.com

The companion devotional books

Dare to Believe
Dare to Trust
Dear to Walk
Living With the Wind in Your Face
Hidden Riches of Secret Places
"Unshackled" ... To Freedom, Peace, and Hope
Are available at www.amazon.com

You can receive the "Dare Devotions" each day on your computer by clicking www.litmin.org. These devotions are from my first three books and are sent worldwide to thousands of subscribers. There is no cost or obligation to subscribe and receive these devotions each day on the web site. Just get blessed!

Made in the USA
Charleston, SC
06 June 2015